FIND YOUR VOICE

CONQUER YOUR FEARS & SHARE YOUR STORY WITH CONFIDENCE

LESLIE C. FIORENZO

This work is dedicated to my two biggest fans, my daughter, Carla & my husband, Butch. Your support and encouragement means the world to me.

Find Your Voice:

Conquer Your Fears & Share Your Story With Confidence

Disclaimer

The author and publisher have taken great care in compiling all the texts in this book. Nevertheless, errors cannot be ruled out. Liability on the part of the publisher or the author, regardless of the legal basis, is excluded. The reader is solely responsible for all consequences resulting from actions taken on the basis of recommendations in this book.

CONTENTS

INTRODUCTION

OVERCOME YOUR FEAR AND SPEAK WITH CONFIDENCE

Imagine you've been invited to speak to an audience full of your right-fit clients. You're stepping onto a stage and there is a crowd of blank faces filling the seats before you. You step up to the microphone as a bright light shines in your eyes. You're ready. You practiced your words all night. Your index cards are stacked neatly on the podium before you.

And then it hits you.

This isn't just a small tremor of anxiety; it's a full-blown earthquake, shaking your confidence to the core. The thought of public speaking leaves your palms slick with sweat, and your voice trembling. The camera becomes a judgmental eye, exposing every perceived flaw. Networking events morph into social minefields, filled with potential rejection.

These fears silence your voice, the very message that

could resonate with your ideal clients and propel your business forward. You know visibility is key, yet the fear holds you hostage, whispering insidious doubts:

- "Who am I to speak in front of others?"
- "They'll see through my facade and judge me."
- "What if I make a mistake?"

The silence becomes deafening. Opportunities slip away, replaced by a gnawing sense of "what if?" You yearn to share your expertise, connect with your audience, and watch your business flourish. But the fear binds you, leaving you frustrated and unfulfilled.

The Impact:

This fear doesn't just stifle your voice; it:

- **Limits your reach:** Your ideal clients remain unaware of your offerings, leading to missed opportunities and stagnant growth.
- **Breeds self-doubt:** The constant battle with fear erodes your confidence, impacting your overall well-being and motivation.
- **Hinders connection:** By staying in the shadows, you miss the chance to build meaningful relationships with clients and potential collaborators.
- **Thwarts growth:** Your business remains

invisible, limiting its potential for impact and expansion.

My goal is to help you overcome that fear, and its limits and help you share your story in a powerful and meaningful way.

I've always felt a strong pull towards connecting with others. One of my earliest memories, before the age of 4 stands out vividly. I went into the year of a church next door and, with the innocence of a child, stood at the door where the kids were leaving Sunday school, declaring, "Shake hands with Leslie Broas." (my maiden name) and while the adventure got me in a bit of trouble with my parents who were unaware of my whereabouts, it was a clear sign of my innate love for people and being in front of them.

For me, the stage never presented itself as a source of fear but rather as a bridge to connect. Yet, the art of public speaking is one that requires sharpening and practicing your craft. A fact I learned through both humbling and enlightening experiences. In my early twenties, I joined a women's organization BPWUSA. In addition to the local chapter meetings, there were opportunities for regional, state, and national meetings and activities. At one point the West Michigan region offered a speaking contest. I remember participating in a speaking contest, I entered full of confidence and certainty. Wow, was I disappointed when I didn't even place in the top 5 out of 30 contestants.

The feedback I received, however, was valuable even though it left me on the brink of tears. I felt like I had put a lot of energy and effort into the presentation, and yet I didn't qualify to move onto the state level. It was a pivotal moment that made me realize the need to improve.

Lucky for me I had a great mentor in Louise Cole. She was a long-time member probably 20 years my senior and took me under her wing. She saw potential in me that I had yet to fully realize and guided me toward nurturing it. She helped me understand that presentations needed to be more than facts and data. Her sage advice would alter the course of my speaking abilities. This guidance was the first step in a transformative journey that would see me join the ranks of Toastmasters. If you're not familiar with Toastmasters, it's a remarkable organization dedicated to helping individuals overcome their fear of public speaking. It provides a supportive environment where you can practice, receive feedback, and learn to speak off the cuff with confidence.

Toastmasters proved to be an invaluable experience. It allowed me not only to craft and present prepared speeches but also to respond to impromptu topics with poise. Alongside the support from mentors and the nurturing environment of Toastmasters, I learned another crucial lesson: the importance of investing in oneself. This investment isn't merely financial—it's about dedicating time, energy, and effort to develop your skills as a speaker. I dove into this pursuit wholeheartedly, and it has paid dividends in ways I couldn't have imagined. The book you are now reading is one of those dividends.

Whether it's reading books on communication, attending workshops, or simply practicing your speech in front of a mirror, every bit counts. With each step you take, you're building not just your speaking prowess but also your self-confidence. And believe me, the audience can sense that confidence. It's infectious, and it transforms the way they receive your message.

I have found it helpful to have a partner in your journey of self-improvement. That could be hiring a coach to help or enlisting a friend or colleague to read this book and meet up once a week to discuss what you've learned. This other person is often referred to as an accountability partner. Throughout my life, as I've wanted to grow and improve, I've found true value in joining forces with someone supportive, who will listen and encourage me and also ask, when appropriate, what you learned about yourself when you failed to keep your commitment for the week.

My guess is you purchased a copy of this book because you are grappling with the fear of public speaking, knowing that it's a mountain that can indeed be conquered. It may seem daunting from the foothills, but with each stride, you'll find the path clearer and your load lighter. Remember, every great speaker was once a beginner, and every expert has a tale of obstacles they've overcome. Be patient with yourself, seek support, embrace growth, and most importantly, keep connecting with those around you. Your voice has power and people need to hear your story.

A poem entitled Our Deepest Fear has always resonated with me. It is from the book "Return to Love" by Maryanne Williamson.

Our deepest fear is not that we are inadequate.
Our deepest fear is that we are powerful
beyond measure.
It is our light, not our darkness
That most frightens us.
We ask ourselves
Who am I to be brilliant, gorgeous, talented,
fabulous?
Actually, who are you not *to be?*
You are a child of God.
Your playing small
Does not serve the world.
There's nothing enlightened about shrinking
So that other people won't feel insecure
around you.
We are all meant to shine,
As children do.
We were born to make manifest
The glory of God that is within us.
It's not just in some of us;
It's in everyone.
And as we let our own light shine,

We unconsciously give other people permission
to do the same.
As we're liberated from our own fear,
Our presence automatically liberates others.

There are two key phrases that I want to point out here. First, it is our light, not our darkness that we are frightened of because we think who am I to be brilliant, gorgeous, talented, fabulous? Each one of us has a purpose to fulfill and playing small or shrinking back does not serve the world in which we are living. You are meant to shine, and I hope that in reading the pages of this book and acting on what you've learned, you will shine brighter than before. Your shining will inspire others to step out of the shadows, make their contribution and we can all contribute to making this world a better place. It is cyclical, my friends, because when we do the work that we are meant to do, it inspires others, and it all comes back around. Commit today to overcoming the fear that is holding you back to get out and share your story either in person or online.

Here is my first recommendation.

1. Get a piece of paper (a sticky note is great for this) and write the following statement:
2. I, (insert your name) commit to finding my voice and sharing my story.
3. Post it in a place where you will see it every day, and read it out loud in the morning and

at the end of the day until you are confident in your ability to speak in person, on camera, or at a networking event.

Yes, this will mean stepping out of your comfort zone and your inner critic will be screaming in your ear. No worries, we will deal with that in chapter 4. For now, remember what Jack Canfield tells us – everything we want is on the other side of fear.

I believe you are reading this book because you are a student of self-improvement. Your investment is more than the price of the manuscript; it is your time and energy in the pursuit of excellence in public speaking. While one can argue only a few people will reach the stature of Oprah, Tony Robbins, or Gary V, I believe self-improvement is a worthwhile endeavor. You may recall the story of Rudy Ruttinger and his determination to play football for the University of Notre Dame. What Rudy lacked in athletic ability he more than made up for in desire and heart. And what's more, he accomplished his goal. He played football for the school he so loved. Please, dear reader, embark on the adventure of self-improvement by doing more than reading the pages that follow. Complete the work suggested in each chapter. Your future self will thank you.

Break Free from the Shackles of Self-Doubt

Do you dream of building a thriving business,

connecting with your ideal clients, and making a real impact in the world? Yet, a nagging fear of self-promotion holds you back. You know you need to put yourself out there, to share your story and expertise, but the thought of public speaking, getting on camera, or networking events sends shivers down your spine.

You're not alone. Countless people find themselves locked in this same struggle. The fear of self-promotion, often filled with anxieties about judgment, inadequacy, and rejection, becomes a silent adversary, whispering doubts and keeping your true potential untapped.

This book is your guide to breaking free. But before we leap into solutions, we will dig deeper into the untold story of self-promotion fear: why it grips so many of us, the unique challenges it presents to solopreneurs, and the common anxieties that hold us hostage.

First, we'll unveil the hidden roots of this fear. We'll explore the psychological barriers, the cultural pressures, and the misconceptions that keep us silenced. You'll recognize your struggles reflected in common narratives and discover you're not facing this alone.

But it's not just about understanding the problem. We'll also shed light on the devastating impact this fear has on your business. Missed opportunities, limited reach, and stifled growth are just the tip of the iceberg. You'll see how overcoming this hurdle isn't just about personal triumph; it's the key to unlocking your business's true potential.

Get ready to confront your fears head-on and

embark on a journey of self-discovery. By facing the "why" behind your anxieties, you'll be armed with the knowledge and understanding needed to move forward. The path to a confident, empowered you, and a thriving business, begins here.

Next, we'll shift gears, focusing on the immense power your unique story holds. You'll discover how storytelling is not just about entertainment; it's a powerful tool for:

- Building trust and connection: By sharing your authentic journey, you create deeper bonds with your audience, establishing yourself as a trusted expert.
- Differentiation and memorability: In a crowded marketplace, your unique story sets you apart, making you unforgettable and resonating with your ideal clients.
- Emotional engagement: Stories tap into our emotions, triggering action and motivating your audience to connect with you and your offerings.

I'll share real-life examples of how people used storytelling to skyrocket their businesses, showcasing the tangible results this approach can deliver. You'll gain practical tips and techniques for crafting compelling narratives that resonate with your audience and move them to action.

And in the final part we'll embark on a journey of self-discovery. Through interactive exercises and prompts, you'll:

- Uncover your core values and beliefs: What drives you? What makes your work meaningful? These insights form the foundation of your authentic story.
- Identify your unique experiences and challenges: Your journey, filled with triumphs and obstacles, shapes your perspective, and sets you apart.
- Create your brand narrative: Learn how to weave these threads into a compelling story that resonates with your ideal client, attracting them to your message and offerings.

By the end of this chapter, you'll have a clear understanding of your unique story and the tools to share it with confidence. You'll be ready to step out of the shadows, connect with your audience on a deeper level, and watch your business grow. Be sure to visit my website for free information and downloads. https://www.lesliefiorenzo.com/book/resources

Set an appointment with yourself, preferably at the same time each day over the next few weeks to read the material, reflect on it, and do the work recommended. Your business is important, and your message is important, so investing the time and energy to create a story to share is a worthwhile endeavor. The world needs to hear your message, take the time to make it count. Are you ready to find your voice, conquer your fears, and share your story with the world? Turn the page and let's begin.

PART 1

LAYING THE FOUNDATION FOR SPEAKING SUCCESS

CHAPTER 1

THE UNTOLD STORY: WHY BUSINESS OWNERS STRUGGLE WITH SELF-PROMOTION

> "You may encounter many defeats, but you must not be defeated. In fact, it may be necessary to encounter the defeats, so you can know who you are, what you can rise from, how you can still come out of it." - Maya Angelou

Stories abound with people who have continued to try despite overwhelming odds. Here are a few of my favorite examples: Basketball star Michael Jordan was cut from his high school basketball team. Abraham Lincoln the 16th president of the United States failed over and over again at being elected to public office. Decca Records rejected The Beatles at their 1962 audition, Colonel Harland Sanders of KFC fame took his 11 herbs and spices secret recipe to 1009 before one said yes. Albert Einstein didn't speak until he was 4 years old and failed the entrance exam for the Swiss Federal Polytechnic school located in Zurich. I'm sure by now you're beginning to get the idea. These people didn't take no for an answer and they continued to try and try until they succeeded. Guess what you can embrace the same tenacity. Overcoming public speaking fears is a challenge that many entrepreneurs face and can be conquered with the right strategies. The goal of this guide is to help you conquer that fear allowing you to confidently create video content, present a webinar or workshop about your area of expertise, and succinctly describe your business when networking.

If you are the best-kept secret in town because you are afraid to speak up and talk about your business in person or online the chances of your business growing are slim to none. In today's world creating content for potential clients to consume is paramount. The use of video blogs or vlogs has grown in popularity over the last twenty-plus years. According to a 2022 survey of worldwide consumers they spent an average of 19 hours per week watching online videos.[1] Video marketing statistics on bitable.com show the following:

- Social media posts with video have 48% more views.
- 60% of businesses use video as a marketing tool.
- 50% of marketers who use video have done so for over a year.

- 36% of marketers make videos a few times a week, while 14% make videos every day.

In a 2020 study done by Wyzol, the use of video in marketing strategies rose from 78% in 2015 to 92% in 2020.[2] This same study predicts the average person will spend 100 minutes every day watching online videos, a 19% increase over 2019. What is of additional interest is that almost half (48%) of consumers use videos about a product or service in their purchase decision-making. Tweets that feature video get 10 times the engagement of Tweets that do not contain video.[3]

Chances are you started your business because you wanted to make a difference in the world. Given the data listed above video will continue to play a bigger and bigger role in how businesses engage with prospects and clients. Learning anything new often requires us to step out of our comfort zone. So, as the saying goes, you need to learn to get comfortable being uncomfortable. Consider learning to create video content to market your business a process for self-discovery and improvement. It is an opportunity for growth that requires a commitment to excellence. A recent trend survey of customers done by HubSpot, a favorite customer platform, revealed 78% said it is more important for video to be relatable and authentic rather than polished and high quality.

If you are thinking, "Yeah, but I'm not so sure I can create content that my potential customers want to hear." You need to stop that self-talk and replace language that empowers you to take action. This is my advice on one way to do that. I call it the note to self and a sticky note is ideal for this process. On a sticky note that is at least 2 x 2 inches square and write down the following sentence.

I, (insert your name here) am an amazing speaker and networker. Every day and in every way I'm getting better and better.

Now post it where you can see it every day and repeat it out loud twice a day. Once at the start of your workday and the other time at the end. Do this for at least 30 days until it is part of your routine.

All humans are born with two innate fears: loud noises and falling. The rest, like the fear of public speaking, are learned. The good news? We can unlearn our fear. It can be helpful to understand why we are fearful before we talk about how to overcome it.

Early humans, living in small nomadic tribes, were always on the lookout for danger. The genes of the people who were the best at sensing danger and running away from it were passed down from generation to generation. The genes of those who stopped to enjoy the scenery along the way did not get passed down because they were killed by a wild animal or a neighboring tribe. Fast forward to now and know that your fear of stepping in front of the crowd is founded on this ancient desire for survival. When we speak to an audience, all eyes are upon us. Our brain fires off a message of warning because it thinks those eyes are of an enemy or predator peering out of the bushes with the intent to do us harm.

We also need to understand how judgment played a role in the survival of early people. We needed to stay in the group and abide by group rules. If we were somehow judged unworthy and kicked out of the tribe, death was most likely to occur. We needed to stay in the good graces of the leader and others in the group to survive. Today, when we step out in front of a microphone or hit the record button to create content, our brain warns us about the riskiness of this activity.

Woven in with the fear of judgment is the fear you'll forget your content. You will get behind the microphone to share your message and it will suddenly disappear from your mind, and you'll stammer and stutter and look ridiculous.

Then we are afraid of the critical voice inside our head that says, "Who do you think you are? They'll find out you're a fake" Or the one that says, "Hey, you don't want to look stupid, do you?" Or finally, "No one is interested in what you have to say, you're boring!"

The underlying factor in all of these fears, which I've heard characterized as **F**alse **E**vidence **A**ppearing **R**eal, is our brain simply doing its job - keeping us safe. Guess what, we can retrain our brain and much of the material and activities in this book is designed to help you do that.

Neuroscientists have discovered our brain's ability to

change and grow new pathways, it's called neuroplasticity.[4] Think of it like this. Imagine a field of grass, you are on one side and your destination, let's say a spot by a small stream perfect for sitting quietly and taking time to relax, is on the other side of the field. There is no path, you have to make one. The first time you walk through the grass you'll hardly make a dent. Yet when you walk that same path day after day year after year it will be well-worn and easy to follow. The neural connections in our brain are a lot like creating the path. The first time we have a new thought, the connection is weak, but when we repeat that thought over and over it strengthens that connection. We can also delete old pathways in our brains that no longer serve us. When we think new encouraging thoughts and stop thinking our old discouraging thoughts those pathways will eventually die off. Just like the path to the stream, if we stop going across that field, the grass will eventually grow back and cover it up. One of the reasons I've invited you to create and post notes with new thoughts is to help you create new pathways in your brain to serve you in overcoming your fear.

You can use the following techniques to overcome the fear of speaking in front of people and sharing your story.

It is helpful to remember these fears will not magically disappear, it will take work to overcome them. It is a gradual process, and it's okay to take small steps. That is what I recommend. Take one step every day that scares you. As former First Lady Eleanor Roosevelt once said, "Do one thing every day that scares you. Those small things that make us uncomfortable help us build the courage to do the work we do." It does take courage to stand in front of an audience or record a video for our website or social media post. A worthwhile journey begins with a single step. So the journey of building the courage to speak in front of others is done with small steps repeated daily over time.

TECHNIQUE #1: REFRAME FAILURE AS LEARNING

Research done by American Psychologist, Carol Dwek's on growth versus fixed mindset is helpful here. In her book *Mindset: The New Psychology of Success* she reveals that people with a fixed mindset, believing that abilities are fixed, are less likely to thrive than those with a growth mindset, those who believe abilities can be developed. In a January 13, 2016, Harvard Business Review article she sums up the findings like this: "Individuals who believe their talents can be developed (through hard work, good strategies, and input from others) have a growth mindset. They tend to achieve more than those with a more fixed mindset (those who believe their talents are innate gifts). This is because they worry less about looking smart and put more energy into learning."

Change your view of making mistakes. Instead of

viewing mistakes as failures, see them as opportunities to learn and improve. Embrace the growth mindset, understanding that everyone makes mistakes. Fail simply means **F**irst **A**ttempt **I**n **L**earning. Keep this posted (I do) right next to the sticky note with your commitment to yourself made in the introduction of the book. Visible reminders are helpful tools when we want to make change. We all start somewhere; the important part is to start.

The only impossible journey is the one you never begin. There will never be an exact right time or perfect moment to begin. When we wait for conditions to be just right, we are avoiding making our dreams come true. Embrace the discomfort of the unknown and begin.

Next, choose to focus on the value you are providing. Only you can bring your special gift to the world. Sharing your knowledge and insights with your audience is important. There are people in the world that need to hear your message. They are waiting to purchase the programs you offer. No one else can share your message in the way you can because they have not had your unique set of experiences. If one method doesn't work, try something else,

At one point in my life I joined a home-based direct sales company. The woman who enrolled me on her team suggested I create a piece of paper with 100 squares on it. I could only mark an X in the square when someone said "No" to booking a party with me.

That was a method she used to build her successful home-based business. It is because many of us tell ourselves a story about that word ***no***. It means failure and rejection. Let's reframe it. The more potential customers that tell us no, the closer we are to a yes. Take a few minutes right now and create a "no" sheet for yourself. Put your name and today's date at the top with the heading 100 No's then create a table with 100 squares.

TECHNIQUE #2: VISUALIZE SUCCESS

Many times we create a picture in our head filled with worst-case scenarios. Instead of awfulizing the events in your life, see them going well. One more interesting factoid about your brain - it does not know the difference between what is happening and what we imagine. When we mentally rehearse things going well, we begin to build the neural pathways to achieve that success. Performers like Jim Carrey and Arnold Schwarzenegger and athletes like Michale Phelps and Connor McGregor have used visualization methods to launch them into stardom. And you can too. Here's what to do:

Set a timer for 3 minutes. Close your eyes and sit in a comfortable position with your feet flat on the floor. Take a long slow inhale in (count of 3) and a long slow exhale out (count of 3). Next, visualize a supportive and engaged audience that wants you to succeed. If your event is in person In your mind's eye see the audience smiling and nodding with your words. Hear the applause after your speech, maybe even imagine a standing ovation. If the event is virtual, see the friendly faces on camera connecting with your message. See the chat box full of positive comments. They are engaged and want to hear more from you. The event host comments this is one of the best presentations the group has ever experienced. Feel the feelings you would if this was happening in real life. Once the timer goes off, stay in that moment and revel in success.

This visualization technique can be used anytime you want to picture yourself succeeding at any activity personally or professionally.

TECHNIQUE #3: CREATE COMPELLING CONTENT

No one sets out to be boring and yet, I'm certain, you've heard many boring presentations in your lifetime. The best way to overcome the fear of being boring is to craft your content to be engaging and relevant. When you sit down to create your content keep 3 things in mind:

- KISS- Keep it sweet and simple. Our attention spans these days are growing shorter and shorter. I've heard it compared to that of a goldfish and the goldfish's attention span is longer! Anyway, the trend of creating short bite-sized pieces of content, especially for

social media is growing so this can be a good thing to keep in mind.
- Facts tell - stories sell. I may or may not remember your statistics. Tell me a story and I will remember it because a good story makes a human connection and elicits emotion in the listener. One of my clients did when she reviewed her proposal with a prospect. For each data point in her presentation, she had a story. Guess what? She landed the biggest contract in her business to date.
- Never make a point without a story and never tell a story without a point. This was the mistake I made in my first ill-fated speaking contest. I told a bunch of stories that didn't relate to any point I wanted to make.

Before you sit down to develop your message, be sure you have a good understanding of your audience's interests. In addition to knowing the demographics (age, gender, race, geographic location) of your audience, understand the psychographics (personality, values, attitudes, interests, and lifestyle). By starting here you can tailor your content to resonate with them. A well-researched and audience-centric presentation is more likely to be interesting.

You will want to answer the following questions about your audience:

1. What do they already know about my topic?
2. What can I say that is a different way of looking at what they already know?
3. What story illustrates my point?
4. What emotional connection do I want to create?
5. What action do I want them to take as a result of listening to the presentation?

Use your answers to create your presentation bulleted outline containing the key points. Then go back and fill in the sub points. Once you have your content, it is time to rehearse.

TECHNIQUE #4: PRACTICE EQUALS CONFIDENCE

Almost every bottle of shampoo comes with instructions to lather, rinse, and repeat. The same is true for your presentation. Say the words out loud and say it again. Repetition is the mother of all learning. There is no hard and fast rule for the number of times you need to rehearse; thoroughly practicing will build confidence in your knowledge of the material. Rehearse until you know the key points of your message by heart; it will bolster your confidence.

Consider setting up a practice space. If your event is in person, set up a few chairs in front of you to simulate the feel of the room. You may want to fill the chairs with "people" faces from magazines, stuffed animals, or dolls borrowed from your child's toy box. As you rehearse you can practice making eye contact with this imaginary audience. If it is a virtual event, use a platform like Zoom or Google Meet and practice. No one will see this; it is just a space for you to practice.

The more prepared you are, the more your message will have a positive impact. Remember, your audience is seeking the change your story has to offer, that is why they attended your event or signed up to receive your content.

Incorporate visual aids, slides, or cue cards to provide additional support. Tools like this can help you stay on track if you momentarily forget a specific point. If you decide to create a slide deck, use a few words on the slide and more pictures. In the English language, we read from left to right. Consider putting your visual on the left side of the screen and the words on the right side of the slide. Your audience will be reading the slide, so the fewer words the better so they listen to you. A little more brain science here, we cannot listen and read at the same time. We will get about 50% of both and that will not equal 100% of the message.[5] Make it easy for your audience to listen to you. Use pictures that relate to your message and a few words on the screen.

TECHNIQUE #5: AVOID SEEKING APPROVAL

The vast majority of audiences are empathetic and supportive. Yes, there is an occasional negative Nancy that you can ignore. People show up to gain insights from your presentation, not to criticize or disagree. Concentrate on delivering your message rather than seeking constant approval. Shift your focus from self-judgment to the importance of the information you're sharing. Yes, your message may not land with everyone and that's okay. Embrace the comments from your audience, both positive and constructive, as a means of improvement. Remember to pursue excellence, not perfection. One of my favorite quotes on this subject is by Emerson: "Finish each day and be done with it. You have done what you could. Some blunders and absurdities no doubt crept in; forget them as soon as you can." It is true of any presentation as well. He continues, "Tomorrow is a new day. You shall begin it serenely and with too high a spirit to be encumbered with your old nonsense."

Keep a feedback journal. After every time you speak, in person or virtually answer the following questions.

- What went well (where did I succeed)?
- What did I learn?
- What will I do differently next time?

Ask your audience for feedback. Create a comment card for your audience to use. It can look something like this:

Name & Date of Presentation

Program Evaluation

What will I implement: ____________________
My thoughts on today's program: ____________________
Thanks! Can I quote you on that? Yes / No
Your name: ____________________
Your title: ____________________
Your email: ____________________
Would you like (insert your name) free gift? Yes / No
What other organization should know about (insert your name) for their next conference or retreat?
Name: ____________________ Title: ____________________
Organization: ____________________
Email: ____________________ Phone: ____________________

One key to getting people to fill out a comment card is to walk them through it at the end of your presentation. Give them step-by-step instructions on filling out the information. It seems counterintuitive yet, but in my experience, I get far better results when I take this one step instead of saying please fill out the comment card on your table.

For virtual events consider a follow-up survey and offer a drawing for a giveaway (like a free 15-minute laser coaching session with you) for all those who submit the survey within 24 hours. Again the point is you want contact information from as many people as possible to grow your list.

Practice consistently, seek constructive feedback, and

celebrate your successes along the way. Consider feedback an essential part of the learning process. Each positive experience will contribute to building your confidence as a public speaker.

The five techniques covered in the last part of the chapter are designed to build a foundation for creating your story and speaking success. Let's add some additional information.

This world is filled with things over which we have no control. There are, however, three things we can always control: our thoughts, our actions, and our focus. What if we gave up trying to control things over which we have no control and focused solely on the things over which we do have control? Life would be a lot less stressful and a lot more fun. This final section of the chapter will focus on the change over which we have control - our focus, our body, and our self-talk. Think of it as the three C's of change. When we take the time to do these three things it will allow us to instantly feel differently and be ready to take action.

CHANGE YOUR FOCUS

> "Energy flows where focus goes" - Tony Robbins

Our attention acts like a spotlight, illuminating what we choose to see. Instead of focusing on negativity or limitations, train your focus on possibilities and solutions. Journal your answers to the following empowering questions: "What are the opportunities in this situation?" "What resources do I have to overcome this challenge?"

Use breathing techniques to help you regain focus. Breathe into the count of four, hold your inhale for four counts, exhale to the count of four then hold your exhale for four counts. I shared this method in a social media post recently and had someone I had not seen in several years comment in a direct message to me "I used your breathing exercise reminder video last week for something. It was helpful!!!"

Practice mindfulness exercises like meditation or spending time in nature to improve your ability to redirect your focus intentionally. Use your 5 senses to help you take a break and reduce feelings of anxiety or stress. Here are the general directions:

- Notice five things that you can see. Look around you. ...
- Notice four things that you can feel. Tune in to your sense of touch. ...
- Notice three things you can hear. Listen carefully. ...
- Notice two things you can smell. Notice and name two smells you recognize.
- Notice one thing you can taste.

No judgment is necessary, just notice what is

happening using your 5 senses to be present in the moment.

CHANGE YOUR BODY

"It's going to be a journey. It's not a sprint to get in shape." - Kerri Walsh Jennings

Our physical state deeply impacts our mental well-being. When feeling anxious or down, adopt power poses like standing tall with shoulders back and hands on your hips or raised above your head in victory.

Engage in physical activity: a brisk walk, a yoga pose like a down dog or legs up the wall, or even jumping jacks can release endorphins and shift your mood. Even small changes like sitting up straight or taking deep breaths can boost your energy and confidence.

Have a dance party and use music to improve your state. Put on the music that makes you feel how you want to feel. What songs make you come alive? I keep a playlist that includes Eye of the Tiger by Survivor, Roar by Katy Perry, I Won't Back Down by Tom Petty, Don't Stop Believin' by Journey, Shake It Off by Taylor Swift, and the theme from Rocky starring Sylvester Stallone.

Using a breathing technique like boxed breathing can change how we are feeling in our bodies. Sit comfortably in your chair, feet flat on the floor, breathe into the count of 4, hold your inhale for 4 counts, exhale for 4 counts and hold your exhale for 4 counts. As you breathe in, visualize a line going up in a vertical direction. As you hold your inhale the line goes across to the right. As you exhale the line goes down even with the line that went up on the inhale. As you hold your exhale the line goes across on the bottom completing the square or the outline of a box. Do this a half dozen times and feel the relaxation flow into your body.

CHANGE YOUR SELF-TALK

"The more a man meditates on good thoughts, the better will be his world and the world at large." - Confucius

The inner voice is powerful, and often our harshest critic. Become aware of your self-talk and replace negative narratives with positive affirmations. Instead of saying "I can't do this," shift to "I'm capable of learning and growing." Treat yourself with compassion and encouragement, just as you would a friend facing a challenge.

Have you ever noticed the words you choose to say after the phrase "I am" reinforce your feelings? For example, when you say, I am tired, you feel more tired. When you say; I am frustrated, feelings of frustration are compounded. Similarly, when you say, I'm so upset, you will add the feeling of being dismayed. Start paying attention to the words you say after you say "I am" and change them into strong powerful statements. Here are some positive phrases to use: I am successful. I am talented. I am confident. I am focused.

One remarkable resource that was super helpful to

me was Dr. Shad Helmsetter's book "What to Say When You Talk to Yourself" You can find it on Audible and Amazon. Of course, you can put some prompts into an AI resource like ChatGPT or Google's Gemini. Whatever the method you choose, pay attention to that voice in your head and use it to create good.

Remember, change takes time and effort. Be patient and celebrate small victories. By consistently focusing on these three areas, you'll build a foundation for resilience, positivity, and empowered action.

I love the advice Jerry Seinfeld gave an up-and-coming comedian about improving his joke-telling ability. He said to get a big wall calendar and every day you write jokes for 15 minutes and make a big red X on the date. Soon you will have a chain of X's. Don't break the chain. You can use a similar tool to help you begin to overcome your fear.

ACTION STEP

- Start small: Pick one action from each area (e.g., focus on gratitude for 5 minutes, do 10 jumping jacks, replace one negative thought with a positive one) and practice them consistently.
- Track your progress: Journaling about your shifts in focus, body language, and self-talk

can provide motivation and reinforce positive changes.

- Seek support: Share your journey with a trusted friend, coach, or therapist for encouragement and accountability.

By taking control of your thoughts, actions, and focus, you unlock your potential to create the life you desire.

What is the one action you will take for the next 30 days that will make a difference in overcoming your fear of public speaking, getting on camera, or showing up at a networking event? Write that in the space below:

The action I am committing to for the next 30 days is:

____

____

____

Each day when you take the action make a check mark in the box below.

CHAPTER 2

THE POWER OF YOUR VOICE: WHAT STORYTELLING CAN DO TO FUEL YOUR BUSINESS GROWTH

> "We can't become what we need to be by remaining what we are." - Oprah Winfrey

Growth requires change. Maybe you want to remain a solo practitioner or build a company that you can sell and retire. Building a business requires us to step into who we are meant to be. Creating and sharing your story can power up the growth of your coaching or consulting practice.

Ever since humans have been on planet Earth, we've told stories. The hunters, triumphant from the day's exploits return, and the tribe gathers around the fire to hear the story of what happened. Stories were told over and over again before the written word. Once the printing press came into being, stories became a more indelible part of the fabric of society. Stories are in our DNA. Stories help us make a connection with our ideal client. The key to unlocking powerful connections and business growth lies not in telling your customers facts, but in finding your voice and telling them a story. Yes, storytelling. It's a potent tool for businesses too, and one that doesn't require you to become a polished orator. Think of it as sharing your journey, your struggles, and your triumphs in a way that resonates with your audience.

MAKE A CONNECTION

In a world saturated with information, people connect with emotions, not facts. Stories have the power to build trust and credibility; forge deeper connections; make your message memorable and Inspire action. Let's explore these ideas.

By sharing your authentic experiences, you show your audience that you're a real person with relatable challenges and a genuine passion. You're not just building a bridge to your audience; you're inviting them into your living room. Forget the sterile facade of perfect products and flawless solutions. Instead, peel back the layers and reveal the real you. Share the struggles that made you stronger, the doubts that fueled your determination, the victories that ignited your passion. Let them see the scars of your journey, the stumbles along the path, and the messy, beautiful humanity that lies beneath them. Because it's in that vulnerability, in that shared experience of the human condition, that connection truly takes root. When you show your audience that you're not just a brand or a product, but a fellow traveler on this crazy journey of life, you earn their trust, their respect, and ultimately, their loyalty. Share the real you, and watch your audience transform from strangers into friends, captivated not just by your story, but by the real person telling it. This fosters trust and makes them more receptive to your message.

Stories create emotional bonds, tapping into the very core of what makes us human. When you share your journey, your audience connects with you on a personal level, triggering the release of oxytocin, the "bonding hormone." This deeper connection, rooted in biology, translates to loyal customers and brand advocates who champion your success.

POWERFUL CONNECTIONS THAT BUILT POWERFUL BRANDS.

There are many stories told about company founders and how they impact business growth.

You may be familiar with some of the following products and how the story helped them grow.

1. **Blake Mycoskie and TOMS Shoes:** TOMS Shoes, known for their "One for One" business model where they donate a pair for every pair purchased, wasn't just selling shoes; they were selling a story. Blake Mycoskie, inspired

by witnessing poverty in Argentina, weaved a narrative of giving back and creating positive change through the purchase of a simple product. This resonated deeply with consumers, particularly millennials who valued social responsibility. TOMS' story helped them grow into a multi-million-dollar company and inspired a generation of conscious consumers.

2. **Jessica Honegger and Warby Parker:** Warby Parker, the online eyewear brand, disrupted the industry by offering stylish and affordable glasses. But their story went beyond just price and design. Jessica Honegger, the co-founder, shared a personal story of frustration with overpriced glasses, highlighting the company's mission to make vision accessible and affordable. This resonated with customers, especially young professionals, who appreciated the brand's transparency and commitment to social impact. Warby Parker's story helped them grow rapidly, becoming a leading online eyewear retailer.
3. **Kendra Scott:** Jewelry designer Kendra Scott built her brand not just on beautiful pieces but also on a powerful story. She openly shared her struggles with infertility and her journey to success, showcasing resilience and authenticity. This resonated with women who

saw themselves in her story and connected with her brand on a deeper level. Scott's story helped her build a loyal community, driving significant growth and creating a strong brand identity.

4. **Yvon Chouinard and Patagonia:** Patagonia, the outdoor apparel brand, is known for its commitment to environmental activism and social responsibility. They regularly share stories of their employees, athletes, and customers who embody these values, creating a strong emotional connection with their audience. While not a single viral moment, this consistent storytelling approach has helped build Patagonia's brand loyalty and attract customers who share their values.

Facts fade, but stories stick. By weaving your brand message into a compelling narrative, you ensure it lingers long after the audience encounters it. It's like the difference between a dry lecture and a captivating novel. The lecturer might recite facts, figures, and statistics, but they often evaporate like mist on the lake. The novelist, however, crafts a tapestry of emotions, experiences, and characters that resonate with the reader, leaving an indelible mark long after the last page is turned.

This is the power of storytelling for your brand. It's not about bombarding your audience with features and benefits, but rather inviting them on the journey of your brand. Telling a story is more than entertainment; they are about connection, about building trust, and about creating a lasting impression. So, ditch the dry facts and embrace the power of storytelling. Let your brand message become a captivating narrative that sticks long after the encounter, leaving your audience not just informed, but truly inspired. Whether it's signing up for your service, purchasing a product, or joining your community, a well-crafted story can motivate your audience to take the next step.

Now you might be thinking I'm no good at storytelling. Relax, storytelling isn't about crafting a best-selling novel. It's about sharing your experiences, passions, and values engagingly. Think about the way advertisers use TV commercials, they most often tell a story. Stories connect us with another person and your client is another person. Yes, maybe you sell your product or service business to business but there is still a human being making that buying decision.

STORYTELLING TECHNIQUES

Use the following storytelling methods, designed to effortlessly ignite your creative process.

- What is your story? Share your unique experiences, challenges, or successes that define your business journey. What drove you to start your business? What motivates you every day? What are the biggest challenges you've faced and how have you overcome them? Sharing your purpose gives your audience a deeper understanding of your brand.

- Focus on the journey, not just the destination. Don't shy away from sharing challenges you've faced and lessons you've learned. These honest moments resonate with your audience and showcase your resilience. One of my favorite rags-to-riches stories is that of Sylvester Stallone. Once he created the scene play for "Rocky" he focused all his time and energy on connecting with people who would make it into a movie. He was turned down time and time again. He was financially bankrupt. He sold his possessions to keep himself and his wife afloat, one of those being his dog! Yet he persisted. And of course, we now know the end of the story. His persistence paid off, and that is the lesson I've taken away from his personal story. Weave a narrative that starts with your origin, the challenges you faced, the hurdles you leaped, and the impact you've made.
- Tailor your story to resonate with the needs and interests of your ideal client. Speak the language they understand and sprinkle in

personal anecdotes to illustrate your points. If your right-fit clients are accounts and CPA they use a language of numbers and details. On the other hand, if your ideal customer is a fashion designer, the words they may use evoke color and imagination. As you have conversations with the people you are serving, pay attention to the words they use to describe their wants, needs, and desires. Incorporate what they are saying to you to create a story that connects.

Humans are creatures of emotion so share stories that evoke feelings like joy, inspiration, or empathy. Did your product help a struggling artist finally express their vision? Did your service empower a local community? Did your journey itself embody resilience and innovation? Let your passion shine through, and prospects won't just remember your features; they'll remember the feeling your story evoked, a feeling that resonates long after the presentation ends and lays the foundation for a deeper connection. Let your enthusiasm ignite a spark in their hearts, let your vulnerability create trust, and let your unique journey show them why you, and not your competitor, are the one they should invest in.

Remember, people buy not just products, but the stories behind them – stories that make them feel something.

You probably have a supply of sticky notes in your home or office. The origin story of this ubiquitous product is anything but ordinary. In the late 1960s, Arthur Fry, a 3M scientist, sang in a church choir. Frustrated by losing his hymnal bookmarks, he dreamt of a repositionable adhesive that wouldn't damage delicate paper. After years of trial and error, the "Press-n-Peel" notecard was born. It was met with initial skepticism. It wasn't until a secretary at 3M, frustrated by losing phone messages, saw its potential. Word spread and the rest is sticky note history.

You or your child may have a fidget spinner. This product was created by a busy teacher, constantly battling restless students who doodled, fidgeted, and struggled to focus. Frustrated by traditional methods, she started brainstorming. Inspired by fidget toys designed for children with ADHD, she envisioned a simple, non-disruptive tool that could subtly channel excess energy for everyone. Thus, the fidget spinner was born. Sure your product or service has not seen that type of notoriety yet. What was the motivation behind your business beginning? There is a story there to tell.

The most impactful stories are those delivered with genuine enthusiasm. Forget perfectly polished presentations and meticulously crafted narratives. Forget the dry recitation of features and benefits. Stories that connect with your audience resonate with an infectious energy that speaks volumes even beyond spoken words. Speak of the moment you first glimpse the potential of your product, the thrill of overcoming a seemingly insurmountable challenge, and the joy of witnessing a client's success story. Let your voice tremble with excitement, your eyes sparkle with conviction, and your entire being radiate the fire that burns within you. Remember, people connect with authenticity, not perfection. Embrace your vulnerability, and let your passion be your guide. Share your story with the fervor that burns within you. That's the power of genuine enthusiasm. It's the difference between a passing glance and a captivated audience, between a transaction and a lifelong connection.

Don't be afraid to experiment and refine your story until it feels authentic and engaging. Think of it as sculpting, chipping away at the rough edges until your unique voice and message emerge. Embrace the messy first draft, the awkward phrasing, and the tangents that lead nowhere. These are your stepping stones, your raw material. Play with different angles, infuse humor or vulnerability, and see what resonates. Test your story on friends, colleagues, or even strangers. Listen to their feedback, not just the words, but the emotions it evokes.

- Does it spark curiosity?
- Ignite excitement?
- Tug at their heartstrings?

If not, refine, rewrite, and try again. Remember, authenticity is crafted and honed through experimentation. The more you experiment, the closer you get to a story that resonates deeply with your audience, leaving them not just informed but truly captivated.

STEP INTO THEIR SHOES

You've heard the expression about walking a mile in someone else's shoes. This applies when it comes to creating a story to share with your right-fit client. Often, coaches or consultants initiate their businesses to serve the communities to which they belong. In this case, they know the struggles of their client because these struggles were theirs. Even if this is not the case you can do some research and discover the answer to the proverbial question: what keeps your client up at night? The more specific you can be, the better connection you will make. This idea is counter-intuitive , especially to new entrepreneurs, because it feels limiting. There is power in focus. Think of the difference between an LED light bulb and a laser beam. Both give off energy, yet the laser beam has the power to cut through steel. You want to harness that same power in the story you tell about your business. Remember, to be terrific you need to be specific.

YOUR GUIDE TO DEVELOPING EMPATHY

Create your story in the context of audience understanding. There are a variety of ways to do this: active listening techniques, empathetic questioning, and observational skills,

LISTEN WITH THE INTENT TO LEARN, NOT JUST TO RESPOND.

This simple shift in mindset can unlock a gold mine of insights and connections in your conversations. Imagine each conversation as a treasure hunt. Sure, facts and figures might be glittering baubles, but the true gems lie hidden in the emotions – the joy, the frustration, the fear, the hope. Stop waiting for that pause, that perfect moment to interject your brilliant idea. Instead, lean in, become a sponge, and listen for the emotion behind the words. What anxieties lie beneath the surface? What hopes and dreams fuel their excitement? By digging deeper into the emotional landscape, you'll discover hidden gems of understanding that facts alone can't reveal.

Suppose you are in a conversation with a potential client. Instead of focusing on their pain points as mere sales opportunities, listen for the frustration, the fear, and the yearning for a solution. By acknowledging their emotional state, you instantly build rapport and trust. You shift from a salesperson to a trusted advisor, someone who understands their needs on a deeper level. This shift unlocks a world of possibilities, allowing you to tailor your message to resonate with their heart, not just their head.

This applies not just to business, but to every interaction. Listening to the emotion behind the words allows you to connect with friends, family, and even strangers on a more meaningful level. You'll discover shared experiences, hidden vulnerabilities, and unexpected depths of understanding. It's like unlocking a secret language, one where empathy and connection flow freely.

Think of it like this: When you listen solely for the break to share your idea, you're like a conductor desperately trying to fit every instrument into the same melody. But when you listen to the emotions, you become an orchestra conductor, harmonizing each instrument, creating a beautiful and dynamic symphony that resonates with everyone involved.

EMPATHIC QUESTIONING.

In today's bustling world, where information flows freely and advice seems readily available, the true magic lies not just in what you say, but in how you listen. At the heart of meaningful interactions, nestled between data and strategies, lies the powerful tool of empathic questioning.

Forget the rapid-fire interrogation, the impersonal probing for facts and figures. Empathic questioning is a fine art, a dance of curiosity and compassion. It goes beyond the surface, seeking to understand the emotions that are underneath a client's experiences, the perspectives that shape their decisions, and the values that guide their aspirations.

Imagine each question as a key, gently unlocking the doors to a hidden chamber within your client. With each thoughtful inquiry, you gain access to their unique emotional landscape, their hopes and fears, their struggles, and triumphs. This deeper understanding fosters trust, builds rapport, and lays the foundation for truly transformative conversations.

Empathic questioning isn't just about gathering information; it's about creating a safe space for exploration, a stage where vulnerability is embraced, and growth becomes possible. By asking open-ended questions, actively listening to their responses, and reflecting to your client their emotions, you become not just a consultant or coach, but a trusted guide on their journey of self-discovery.

Remember, the most powerful questions aren't always the loudest or most complex. Sometimes it can be just one word. A coaching friend of mine tells a story about a client telling him a story about how everyone at the office hated her. The question he asked was one word - everybody? Allowing her to recognize it was not everyone, it was two people. Often, it's the simple, sincere inquiry, delivered with genuine interest, that resonates most deeply. So, the next time you find yourself in a client interaction, silence the urge for immediate solutions and instead, pick up the key of empathic questioning. You might be surprised at the transformative conversations it unlocks, not just for your clients, but for yourself as well.

IMPROVE YOUR POWERS OF OBSERVATION.

In a world saturated with noise and information overload, it's easy to fall victim to the tyranny of the obvious, overlooking the subtle whispers hidden in plain sight. We flit from screen to screen, conversation to conversation, often missing the rich tapestry of non-verbal cues - body language, facial expressions, and gestures that speak volumes beyond words.

Imagine a conversation as a play, where words are the script, but the true performance unfolds in silent exchanges. A furrowed brow betrays hidden worry, a crossed arm indicates resistance and a genuine smile speaks volumes of trust. You may have witnessed two colleagues discussing a project. One leans in, eyes sparkling with genuine interest, while the other fidgets, avoiding eye contact. While their words might convey agreement, their non-verbal cues paint a different picture. By tuning into these often-overlooked signs, we unlock a deeper understanding, fostering more meaningful connections and navigating even the most complex interactions with greater clarity.

Picture a conversation as a dance. The words are the steps, but the body language is the rhythm, the facial expressions are the accents, and the gestures are the flourishes. By focusing solely on the steps, we miss the richness and complexity of the performance. But by paying attention to the entire dance, we gain a deeper appreciation for the artistry and emotion behind it.

GIVE YOUR AUDIENCE A FACE

Creating a powerful story that will resonate with your right-fit client requires more than a broad understanding of your target audience; it demands a deep understanding that goes beyond demographics and statistics. We are going to dive into the idea of crafting audience personas—a powerful tool that is more than demographics; it is putting a face and a story to the data. By visualizing specific individuals within your target audience, you unlock a gateway to tailored communication that resonates on a personal level. This isn't just about reaching a collective; it's about connecting with individuals. To guide you through this process, here is a step-by-step guide and template, equipping you with the tools to create vivid audience personas that breathe life into your communication strategy. Let's unravel the art of putting a face to your audience and, in doing so, elevate the impact of your message.

DEFINE YOUR OBJECTIVES

Clearly outline the goals and objectives of your story. What do you aim to achieve by connecting with your audience? Define the desired outcomes to guide the persona creation process. Before crafting your communication approach, it's crucial to define what you want to achieve by connecting with your audience. This clarity sets the stage for persona development and guides your messaging to resonate effectively. Here's how to break it down:

Goals:

- Where are you heading? What is the overall aim of your communication efforts? Is it brand awareness, lead generation, customer engagement, or something else entirely?
- Specificity matters. Avoid vague goals like "increase engagement." Instead, aim for quantifiable targets like "grow social media followers by 20% within 3 months.

Objectives:

- Break down your goals into smaller, actionable steps. These are the concrete actions you'll take to achieve your goals.
- Examples:

- For brand awareness: Objective 1: Secure media coverage in 3 relevant publications. Objective 2: Increase website traffic by 10% through social media campaigns.
- For lead generation: Objective 1: Generate 100 leads through a webinar series. Objective 2: Increase conversion rates on landing pages by 5%.

Desired Outcomes:

- What impact do you want your communication to have? What do you want your audience to feel, think, or do after engaging with your message?

Examples:

- Feel: Informed, empowered, inspired, connected.
- Think: Your brand is reliable, innovative, trustworthy.
- Do: Subscribe to your newsletter, visit your website, and purchase your product.

IDENTIFY KEY DEMOGRAPHICS

Begin with fundamental demographic information such as age, gender, location, and occupation. Basic demographics like age, gender, income level, location, and education provide a starting point for understanding your audience, but it's important to consider using additional data and segmentation techniques to gain deeper insights into your audience. Be sure to use basic demographics responsibly and ethically, respecting privacy and avoiding discrimination.

EXPLORE PSYCHOGRAPHICS

Dive deeper into the psychographic aspects, including interests, values, hobbies, and lifestyle choices. Understand what motivates and resonates with your audience on a personal and emotional level. Psychographic information helps you understand what motivates them, what resonates with them on an emotional level, and ultimately, what drives their actions. By uncovering their passions, beliefs, and aspirations, you can craft messaging and campaigns that truly connect with them on a personal level. For example, if you know your audience values authenticity, showcase the real people behind your brand. If they're passionate about adventure, create content that inspires them to explore. This deeper understanding will empower you to craft messaging that resonates with their hearts and minds, ultimately driving engagement, loyalty, and conversions.

ANALYZE BEHAVIOR PATTERNS

Demographics and psychographics paint a valuable picture, but truly understanding your audience requires delving into their behavioral patterns. This is where you move beyond static data and discover the dynamic "how" behind their actions. By analyzing their preferences, habits, and decision-making processes, you gain powerful insights into how they interact with information, engage with your brand, and ultimately make choices.

Unveiling the behavioral tendencies of your audience involves several items from tracking their digital footprint to combining data with empathy. Make a plan to do some research to get to know your ideal client in a way that will endure them to you and your business.

Imagine a bustling city street, each person leaving behind a trail of footprints on the pavement. In much the same way, your audience leaves behind digital footprints as they navigate the online landscape. By analyzing their website behavior, social media interactions, and email engagement, you're essentially following these footprints, gaining valuable insights into their preferences and habits. Just as a skilled tracker can decipher clues from footprints in the wilderness, so too can you decode the digital trails left by your audience, guiding your strategy with precision and insight.

Venture beyond the mere click; delve into the 'why' behind their actions. Examine not just what they click on but the underlying motivations. Identify the content that strikes a chord and comprehend the calls to action that propel them to take the next step. It's in unraveling the intricacies of their decision-making journey within your digital realm that you unearth invaluable insights, illuminating the path to tailored and resonant engagement.

Tune in to their actions; observe their purchase history, discern their patterns of product usage, and listen closely to their interactions with customer service channels. In these actions lie the breadcrumbs of their buying habits and decision-making processes. Tune into these signals, and you gain the ability to craft a message that resonates deeply with their specific needs and preferences, fostering a connection built on understanding and empathy.

Factor in the context; avoid examining and taking apart behavior in isolation. Take into account variables such as the time of day, the device employed, and external events that could sway their choices. Embracing this comprehensive approach unveils a more nuanced understanding of their actions, allowing you to appreciate the subtleties that shape their decisions within the broader spectrum of their circumstances.

Remember, data points are just one piece of the puzzle. Numbers can tell you what someone is doing, but they can't tell you why. While analyzing behavior can be informative, it's crucial to combine that data with empathy to understand the underlying emotions and motivations that drive those actions.

By analyzing behavioral patterns, you gain the power to:

1. **Personalize your approach**: Creating a message and offers that resonate with their specific preferences and needs tailoring your communication style to their comfort level, and addressing any underlying concerns they might have.
2. **Optimize your funnel**: Identify friction points and optimize the customer journey for smoother conversion, creating a seamless experience that fosters engagement and drives conversions.
3. **Unlock the power of prediction**: Leverage historical data to identify patterns and trends, allowing you to anticipate your audience's needs and craft solutions before they even know they need them.
4. **Build stronger relationships**: Understand their motivations and tailor your communication to foster deeper connections that resonate with their unique perspective, fostering genuine connection and mutual trust.

When doing behavioral research prioritize user privacy and responsible data collection practices. Unlocking the secrets of behavioral patterns empowers you to move beyond guesswork and connect with your audience on a deeper, more meaningful level. By understanding their "how," you can craft experiences and messages that resonate with their hearts and minds, ultimately driving engagement, loyalty, and success.

COLLECT FEEDBACK AND INSIGHTS

Avoid guessing! Gather feedback from existing clients or your target audience members. Use surveys, interviews, or social media interactions to gain qualitative insights into their needs, preferences, and challenges. This valuable qualitative data will help you make informed decisions and improve your story. There are a number of ways you can collect this information.

- Survey Monkey has free and paid versions to send questions out to your client list.
- Slido is a platform that lets you create and manage live polls, gathering information from your audience during your event.
- Comment cards are another way to collect information that will yield a deep understanding and will allow you to create a truly customer-centric story.
- Bring together a focus group, in person or online, to seek insight into the world of your audience.

- Follow your clients on social media and see what they are posting or who they are following.

PUT IT ALL TOGETHER

Now that you've taken those steps, create a fictional but realistic persona based on the collected data. Give the person a name, a background story, and a set of characteristics that align with the information gathered. Use all the information you've gathered and write an in-depth description of this ideal client avatar. Enhance the persona by adding visual elements. Include images, illustrations, or symbols that represent the persona. Visualization aids in making the personas more relatable and memorable.

By following the five steps outlined above, you'll not only create vivid audience personas but also cultivate a deeper understanding of the individuals you aim to connect with. This, in turn, enables you to tailor your messages with precision and authenticity. Remember: Storytelling is a journey, not a destination. Embrace your voice, share your story authentically, and watch your business blossom with the power of connection.

CHAPTER 3

IDENTIFYING YOUR UNIQUE STORY: PRESENTING YOUR BRAND NARRATIVE

> "The two most important days in your life are the day you are born and the day you find out why." - Mark Twain

There's a moment in every life journey, often tucked away in the folds of memory, that becomes a defining turning point. It may not have been a grand event, but it was a crossroads where choices were made, lessons learned, and the path forward was irrevocably altered. I call this your signature story. It is a story that you can shrink or expand depending on the need. You can use a part of it as a networking elevator pitch or the full-length version in a client presentation or online webinar. It is an important tool in your business and one you will revisit again and again. This chapter is designed to help you begin powerfully creating your story.

The chances of you being born are 400 billion to one.[1] Not only do you have a unique set of fingerprints, but your outer ear, the iris of your eyes, and your teeth, along with the bumps and ridges on your tongue are yours and yours alone.[2] Need I say more to convince you how unique and special you truly are? If you are thinking – there isn't anything special about me or my story – think again. You are the only one who will ever be born in the history of the universe. The goal of this chapter is to help you discover that story that makes you, you.

START WITH WHY

In 2009 thought leader Simon Sinek published his best-selling book, Start With Why. Admittedly it is a book about leadership, yet his core concept, the Golden Circle, is applicable here. At the center of the circle is the word – Why, the next concentric ring is How and the third is What. Sinek claims most leaders have it backward, they start with the outer ring, the "what" they want to do, and then move inward. His claim is that when we start with the inner ring, the why, we can make a bigger impact with our work. I happen to agree.

Take the time at this moment to write out the answers to the following questions about you and your "why"?

YOUR WHY

1. Why do you feel called to do the work you do?
2. Why is your work important?
3. Why will it make a difference in the lives of the people you serve?

Here are my answers to these questions.

MY EXAMPLE

1. *Creating and running a business is a calling. One I cannot seem to let go of...*
2. *My work is important because it makes a difference in the lives of the clients I serve. I know this because they've told me. They've shared the success in their lives that came after we worked together...*
3. *My work makes a difference because it allows people to share their work in a powerful way in the world. The world needs to know about their work. As I often say, "you can't be the best kept secret in town and grow your business." When I help my clients overcome their fear of public speaking, getting on camera, or network to tell their story, it makes a positive impact in the world.*

Now that you've written down the answers to your why, you can module answer the question: What story demonstrates why your work is important?

Take a few minutes right now to create a list of potential stories you can use.

1. Have a pen & paper or a journal nearby.
2. Relax by doing some boxed breathing.
3. Set a time for 15 minutes.
4. If you want to close your eyes and ask yourself the following question - what story demonstrates why my work is important?
5. Now let your mind drift and write down trigger words or create a mind map so you will remember the story later.
6. When the timer goes off you can continue to write, or you can save this work for building your story. You can also use this method when you are creating a talk or a video and want stories associated with each point you are sharing.

Keep in mind a powerful story connects with your audience and makes an impression in many ways.

CREATE EMOTION

Even short stories, like O Henry's "The Gift of the Magi" create powerful emotional impact in a condensed form.

I can still feel a pang of bittersweetness even years after reading it in junior high. The young couple's sacrifice to give each other the perfect present, despite their own limitations, taught me a powerful lesson about love, selflessness, and the true meaning of giving. This experience is a testament to the enduring impact short stories can have, shaping our understanding of ourselves and the world around us.

SPARK DESIRE

Long before the popularity of YouTube, television production crews along with a host visited faraway places and documented the scenery, food, culture, and climate to encourage people to travel there. Hence a travelog was designed to ignite your wanderlust and transport you to the destination described in the video. They weaved together stunning visuals, captivating narratives, and local insights, painting a vivid picture of the place and its unique offerings. Whether it's vibrant culture, breathtaking scenery, or hidden gems, travelogs evoke a sense of wonder and inspire you to experience the destination for yourself. YouTube is filled with people who are sharing their love of travel, and exploring new places to encourage the listener to visit the place they did. One of my favorites is Kenny & Nell.

INSPIRE ACTION

Change only comes about when we take action. Your audience needs to be moved by your words to create change in their life. James Clear's *Atomic Habits* was one such book that inspired me to take action in some ways. His message is simple, small steps every day (AKA habits) yield big results over time. The only impossible journey is the one we never begin. Action does come before success in the dictionary and in life, too.

Here is an example from history. On May 25, 1961, then US President John F. Kennedy, Jr. said to Congress, "I believe that this nation should commit itself to achieving the goal, before this decade is out, of landing a man on the moon and returning him safely to the earth." The first moon landing took place in 1969. When Kennedy visited NASA before that historical event, he was speaking to the workers there and asked a janitor what his job was. The man replied, "Mr. President, I am helping to put a man on the moon." Kennedy was known for his inspirational and oratory skills and while we may not inspire our audience to ascend into outer space, we can develop the storytelling skills that inspire our audience to take action.

POSITIVE OUTCOME

Contrary to the neatly tied-up bows in fairy tale ends, real life rarely offers clear-cut victories or guaranteed "happily ever after." Instead, it gives us a variety of experiences and valuable lessons. By embracing the lessons garnered from our own "journeys" overcoming life's challenges we equip ourselves to navigate the unforeseen, adapt to ever-changing landscapes, and ultimately, write our own meaningful and fulfilling stories. Taking a lesson and creating a positive outcome we encourage the reader to navigate future obstacles with greater resilience and resourcefulness.

In my own life being fired from a job helped me discover opportunities I did not know existed. I became a member and not long after acquired a leadership role in a company that helped members build their business by word of mouth or referral marketing. Looking back I realize the friendships and experiences I had from 2003 to 2012 would not have happened had I not been asked to leave the role I was comfortable in. What they say is true, often what you think is the worst day in your life turns out to be the best because it propels you to a much better future.

NEW PERSPECTIVE

Help your audience step outside of their perspective and examine the world through a new lens. When we step into your journey, we confront our own biases and broaden our perspectives. *Educated* by Tara Westover published in 2018 is one example. In her memoir, she describes growing up in a survivalist family with limited formal education. She challenges readers to consider the importance of education and the complexities of family dynamics. A classic is Harper Lee's *To Kill a Mockingbird*. Set in the American South the reader sees racism and prejudice through the innocent eyes of a young girl. Lee challenges the readers to confront uncomfortable truths about society and the human condition.

INCLUDE PIVOTAL MOMENTS

The creation of your business and the work you do every day began a journey of self-discovery. It is often, in these moments, we find our truest selves. A moment when you look back and realize it fundamentally changed who you are. These pivotal instances, like hidden gems in the tapestry of our lives, hold the power to unveil the core of our being. Let's uncover these significant moments – the turning points that not only define who we are but also illuminate the path to sharing our authentic stories with the world.

Turning points, those unexpected detours, or pivotal moments, are the brushstrokes that paint the canvas of our being. They are not always heroic moments like winning a competition or facing a tragedy, but rather, often reside in the seemingly mundane. A conversation with a stranger that sparks a new passion, overcoming a personal challenge that reveals hidden strength, or simply the quiet act of choosing kindness in a difficult situation – these are all turning points in their own right.

What makes them significant is their power to shift our perspective, unveil previously unknown facets of ourselves, and shape our values. They become the defining points in our narrative, the experiences that shape how we navigate the world and interact with others. By reflecting on these turning points, we gain a deeper understanding of who we are, what we value, and what experiences have shaped our unique journey. This self-awareness becomes the foundation for sharing our authentic story with the world.

OVERCOMING CHALLENGES

Facing adversity or overcoming a significant obstacle, like a personal loss or a professional setback, can reveal unexpected strengths and depths of character. Sharing how we navigated these challenges inspires others and underscores our personal growth. The 1994 critically acclaimed film, The Shawshank Redemption, is one example. The film tells the story of Andy Dufresne, a man who is wrongly convicted of murder and sentenced to life in prison. Despite the harsh conditions, Andy never gives up hope and eventually finds a way to escape. The film is a powerful testament to the human spirit and the importance of hope.

A coaching friend of mine tells the story of one of his clients who, 15 years ago, had an idea of a retail store dedicated to selling items to owners of dogs. She needed financing and approached 39 banks until one said yes. Many people may have stopped after hearing no 10 times let alone 38. Yes, she persisted and now Must Love Dogs Boutique serves hundreds of pet lovers every year.

EMBRACING TRANSFORMATIVE EXPERIENCES

Stepping outside our comfort zones, whether through travel, new relationships, or pursuing a passion, can broaden our perspectives and challenge our assumptions. By acknowledging these experiences and their impact on our outlook, we enrich our stories and inspire connection with others who have similar journeys. *Wild: A Journey from Lost to Found* by Cheryl Strayed is an example of the idea of accepting change. Her memoir tells the story of the author's solo hike on the Pacific Crest Trail after the death of her mother. Through her journey, she confronts her grief, learns to forgive herself, and rediscovers her strength and resilience.

Tony Robbins tells the story of coaching a young man. This young man had every excuse in the book why he could not succeed in life - no education, no money, no family support. Tony had a serious heart-to-heart talk with him encouraging him to take action anyway, and get a PhD in results, with no formal education needed. As he tells the story you discover this young man was Tony himself, an amazing story of transformation.

DISCOVERING HIDDEN PASSIONS

Unearthing a passion or talent can ignite a sense of purpose and direction. Sharing the path of discovery and how this newfound passion has shaped your life adds authenticity and depth to your story. The poignant novel by Khaled Hosseini, *The Kite Runner,* is an example of the author's discovery of his passion for writing. While the main focus of the story is themes of loyalty and betrayal, writing becomes a way for the author to process his past and find his voice.

A former colleague shared a story about his mother-in-law, who came to visit them soon after her husband passed away. Trying to find a way to entertain her on her visit, the family went to the local mall to look around. They entered a fabric store and as she touched the bolts of cloth something resonated in her, and she purchased a simple pattern and material to make a dress. She is now an accomplished seamstress and is often sought out by friends and neighbors to make special occasion dresses.

DEMONSTRATE TRANSFORMATION

Woven into the tapestry of our lives, transformation is the ever-present thread that binds chapters of self-discovery and growth. Our ability to guide others is rooted in the fertile ground of our own transformative experiences. Dive deep into your personal story of metamorphosis. By reflecting on our own transformations, we not only discover the wellspring of resilience but also illuminate the path to empower those we guide. Peel back the layers of change that have sculpted who you are and who you are becoming.

Our ability to articulate and share our moments of vulnerability and triumphant victories are learning guides for the people we serve. Avoid being shy about sharing these moments with your audience. People want to do business with people they know, like, and trust. Sharing your story is one way to build on this concept. It is similar to the scene in the movie The Wizard of Oz when Toto grabbed the curtain and revealed the man behind the curtain was none other than the great and powerful Oz. "You're nothing but a fraud" exclaimed Dorthy. She and her companions were disappointed that Oz was simply an ordinary man from Kansas, who had lost his way and was doing his best to serve the people of Oz in a way he thought they wanted. What he helped them discover was the power they sought from the wizard already lay within each of them. They didn't need a wizard, they needed to trust their internal guidance to bring about the change they desired.

Remember sharing our transformation is not a solitary victory, but a beacon illuminating the limitless potential within us all. As we put our past selves behind us and embrace new horizons, we realize our journey is not an isolated series of events but threads woven into a tapestry of collective empowerment. When we share our evolution, we create a space for authenticity, allowing others to see the inherent beauty of their transformation. It is an ongoing relationship with growth and development. Change is not a fixed destination but an ongoing dance we embrace with open hearts, forever enriching the world with ever-unfolding stories.

USE YOUR UNIQUE PERSPECTIVE

Our unique perspective acts as a kaleidoscope, shaping how we see the world and, in turn, how we offer transformative guidance. Each of us possesses a distinct lens, forged in the fires of our experiences, passions, and insights. This individuality sets us apart as guides on the path of personal and professional growth. In this chapter, we embark on a journey to understand our unique perspectives. It's not just what we see that matters, but how we see it, and this shapes the very narrative of our coaching philosophy. By navigating the intricacies of our viewpoints, we discover the power of embracing authenticity. By leveraging our singular insights, we can then forge deeper connections with those we guide.

Embracing our unique perspectives empowers us as

guides. As we share our lenses, we create a brilliant spectrum of approaches, offering a wider range of solutions and support for diverse individuals seeking transformation. This synergy not only benefits those we guide in a way that fosters a community of learning and. Ultimately, embracing our unique perspectives becomes not just a point of strength, but a cornerstone for fostering a more diverse, effective, and impactful coaching landscape.

HIGHLIGHT TURNING POINTS

Think about the turning points in your life as the crescendos that define the rhythm of our journey. They are the moments of decision, the forks in the road that set us on new and unexpected paths. Take time to reflect upon these pivotal junctures, to extract the profound lessons embedded within. Turning points are not just plot twists; they are the alchemy of change, where challenges are met with choices, and decisions become the brushstrokes that paint the canvas of our existence.

Turning points in my life of a personal nature include meeting my current husband, the birth of our daughter, entering college, and completing my master's degree as an adult learner. Professionally they include being recruited to an employer where I worked from 1992 until being let go in 2003. Attempting to launch a training and development business and going after any business I thought might bring in revenue. I've often said that during the next ten-year period in my career, I did 5 different part-time jobs trying to make a full-time income and when my former employer came calling, yes the one that fired me, I took the job offer. Then in March of 2020, as a newly minted professional growth coach, I gave my notice to launch a coaching practice with the woman who created the program. Once the world shut down a couple of weeks later, we had to regroup. I was offered a job once again in the EAP field at a company where a former coworker of mine worked. I accepted the offer, yet the desire to own a business never left me. While working full time I filled out my business paperwork with the state of Michigan and began coaching once again.

Your ability to identify and articulate these turning points becomes a beacon for those navigating their crossroads. Through storytelling, we transform these moments of uncertainty into beacons of wisdom, guiding others through the labyrinth of transformation. The beauty lies not just in the turning points themselves, but in our capacity to derive meaning from them – to understand how these instances of choice and consequence shape not only our narratives but also inform the compassionate guidance we extend to others.

Celebrate the richness turning points bring to our stories. Whether marked by triumphs or trials, these moments propel us forward, sculpting our character and fostering resilience. Our ability to illuminate these turning points when sharing our story not only enriches our narrative but also provides a roadmap for those we serve, reminding them that in every choice, in every twist of fate, lies an opportunity for growth and transformation. Treat turning points not as mere plot devices but as the powerful catalysts that propel us toward becoming the inspiring humans we are meant to be.

CONCLUSION

My goal for this chapter is for you to identify your unique story. It is a combination of your personal and professional life unearthing pivotal moments and the transformative threads woven throughout. Each turning point shared, each unique perspective unveiled, becomes a stepping stone on your path to success. Through the power of storytelling, we've not only embraced the authenticity of our experiences but forged a deeper connection with those we guide.

Your story may not resonate with everyone, and that's okay. It will resonate with the people you are meant to serve. What marketers often refer to as **"your tribe"**. It is your ideal client. People who are willing to exchange their money for your expertise. I believe if you've been given an idea for a business you need to act on that sooner rather than later. The calling I've had to create a business that makes a difference in the lives of the people I serve will not go away, even though I've tried a couple of times to go back to a job, what a coaching friend of mine refers to as **J**ust **O**ver **B**roke! I recall a story that an author once told about story ideas. She said when the universe gives you a story idea you must start writing or it will be given to someone else. An idea came to her and she failed to act upon it and write the story. A couple of years later she was talking to a fellow author about his new book. He was writing the story she had been given. She learned a hard lesson, ideas are like slippery fish, once we let go, they don't come back again.

So, dear reader, your story is like that. Grab a hold of what makes you unique, the lessons you have learned because they can ignite the potential for self-discovery within others. May their echoes resonate, guiding both ourselves and those we serve toward a future enriched by the unique lessons inscribed upon our hearts.

SUMMARY

Congratulations my dear reader, you have reached the end of part 1! My hope is that I've furthered your desire to overcome your fear of public speaking and push forward and show up with authenticity, integrity, and presence; so you can speak on any stage, promote your business with absolute certainty, and take your business to the next level. Before you move on, take a few moments to celebrate and review what we've discussed.

FACE YOUR FEAR

It is challenging to look fear in the face and take a leap of faith. Building a business is not for the faint of heart. Yet if you are like me, the idea of embracing a lifestyle of my own making, one with more control than the typical 9 to 5 can ever allow. Fear has a few acronyms, the first

– **False Evidence Appearing Real** stems from the fact that our brain doesn't know the difference between real and present danger or the story we make up about what might happen. Chances are, the story we make up will not come true, yet it stops many people from living the life of their dreams. Please don't let that be you. You are an action taker, you want a better life, or you wouldn't be reading this book. So instead of responding to the situations that scare you with **Forget Everything And Run** choose to **Face Everything And Rise**. Find a good support network. A group of people you can meet with in person or online, who are after the same goals. People, you can discuss ideas with, share wins, and the occasional frustration. Next, hire a coach. If you were going on an expedition to explore an unknown territory you would hire a guide. Someone who knew the lay of the land so to speak so you would not stray from the trail and get hopelessly lost. Think of a coach as a guide through the wilderness of building a business. These two investments will save you a lot of time and heartache.

THE POWER OF STORY

Stories bind us to each other. As a tribal species, we crave the connection to other humans and as business owners, we can use the power of story to create a following for our brand. Think of all the brands you use in your everyday life. What attracted you to that brand in the first place? Most likely it was a story about how their product or service solved a problem in your life. Human beings purchase goods and services for two reasons: want and need. You want to create a powerful story, to create a brand to attract your right-fit client. Remember people buy from people they know, like and trust. A well-designed story can help bridge the gap between unknown and known and facilitate the buying decision.

Tell an authentic tale to create an emotional bond with your audience. Try different techniques to step into the shoes of your customer to create a long-lasting connection. When creating any kind of content for your website, blog or social media keep in mind that facts tell and stories sell. Do your research and uncover the needs and wants of the client. Once you have this deep understanding of the audience you serve it is much easier to create a story that resonates with them.

YOUR STORY IS UNIQUE

At the beginning of the chapter we started with the understanding of why you do what you do. You took the time to answer 3 important questions about your "why". Next you made a list of story ideas as they relate to your "why". These story ideas create emotion, spark desire, inspire action and uncover the challenges faced and problems you've solved. It isn't always about having a "happily ever after", it's about the lessons learned in the journey forward. Your story is told through your perspective, it's a tale of the transformation you've experienced. When you share your experiences, you help your followers see what is possible for them. Stop holding back, people need to hear from you!

PART 2

OVERCOMING THE HURDLES AND BUILDING CONFIDENCE

OVERCOMING THE HURDLES AND BUILDING CONFIDENCE

By now I hope that your confidence is growing because you understand the value of a growth mindset and are using affirmations daily. The feelings of confidence come after stepping up and taking action. Get comfortable being uncomfortable and you will command attention with your presentations. The story you tell yourself becomes your reality. Henry Ford said it best: If you think you can or if you think you can't either way you are right. Our mind has the power to make our life a wonderful place to live or a prison where there is no hope. My sincere hope is that you are choosing to live a life filled with positive energy. A life where you share the message you were born to share.

Facing the camera lens may bring up thoughts of imposter syndrome and pressure to be perfect. Look back at the early work of any social media influencer you follow, and you will recognize we all start somewhere. The goal is improvement, striving for excellence, not perfection. You have an important story to tell, and people are waiting to hear it. Don't deprive your audience of that opportunity.

Anyone with a smartphone can create video content for their website or social media. The technology available to simplify and amplify telling your story is readily available and ever-changing. That makes creating content faster, easier, and less expensive than ever before. Try out new techniques and see what aligns with your brand. Be true to who you are when creating content and mastering the software platforms that align with your message.

Remember you have an important message to share. Your story is unlike anyone else's and only you can tell it. I use two questions to help me stay focused and engaged with the work I do – if not now, when? If not you, who? Building a business requires daily action. While it is true the journey of 1000 miles begins with a single step, the journey won't be complete unless you continue stepping forward each day. I'm not suggesting you never take a day off or enjoy some of the fruits of your labor. The essence of entrepreneurship is the freedom to choose when, where, and how you work. What I am saying is practice and preparation are ongoing.

Think of creating and presenting your story like a play on Broadway. The playwright, director, and actors all have work to do every day before the curtain comes up on opening night. The production will proceed as scheduled, with however many performances have been planned. The show closes and the sequence starts all over again with another production. Presenting your business message to a group, no matter what the size, is similar to preparing for opening night and the run of the show. It takes time, energy, and effort to arrive at the place where the curtain rises, and the show begins. The effort is maintained throughout the performance until the show closes. Each performance may change slightly, modifications made based on input from the director until the curtain falls after each performance.

It is my fervent belief you picked up a copy of this book because you have a desire to share your story with the world. The quickest, easiest, and least expensive way to do that is with a powerful presentation using a simple webcam. Since you've invested time in reading, please take the time to implement the recommendations made in the preceding chapters. Your message is worth sharing!

CHAPTER 4

MASTERING YOUR MINDSET: TURN YOUR INNER CRITIC TO INNER CHAMPION

> "Everything begins from the mind, including change. So, if you want to alter your life, you have to start with your mindset." – Alexi Weaver

Think of your mindset as your mental attitude. Your mental attitude is formed by all your experiences, your education, your upbringing, your background, and culture. It is an accumulation of how you interpret all the events that happened in your life. Events are simply events. Every person on this planet has had things happen in their life that could be thought of as wonderful or catastrophic. It is the story we tell ourselves about the event and the perspective from which we view the event that makes it amazing or tragic. Throughout human history countless stories exist of people who have overcome a variety of calamities and limitations to make an impact in the world. The events that occur in our lives can be a springboard to a new and exciting future.

Imagine you get fired from your job. (Maybe, like me you don't have to imagine because it has happened to you.) What will you say the moment it occurs about the event? You can tell yourself that it is the worst day in your life. Or you can create a story that being fired is the best thing that has ever happened. The choice is yours. You cannot change what happened to you. You can only change how you view what happened in your life. Over the years I've spoken to many people who've lost a job and it is only in retrospect do they see that job loss as an event that improved their life. Avoid waiting until time has passed to look back and shift your perspective. Shift your focus from victim to victor. Ask why did this happen **for** my benefit as opposed to why did this happen **to** me. This simple yet powerful switch in the story we tell about an event makes a big difference in the impact it has on us. Our mindset is a choice we make every day and in every moment.

Many times the biggest challenge we have to an improved mindset is our internal dialogue, often referred to as self-talk. Negative self-talk stands as a formidable roadblock on the path to success, often acting as a silent saboteur of our aspirations. This internal dialogue, filled with self-doubt and criticism, has the power to erode confidence and hinder progress. New entrepreneurs especially, grapple with the impact of their inner critic, affecting not just their ability to articulate their message but also impeding the growth of their businesses. It's a pervasive force that whispers doubts about competence and worthiness, casting a shadow on the pursuit of goals. Recognizing and conquering this inner adversary is paramount for unlocking one's full potential. Through transformative coaching, individuals can rewrite this narrative, replacing self-doubt with self-affirmation and paving the way for unbridled success in both personal and professional realms.

Think of your brain as having 3 parts. The first part is the base or reptilian brain, next is your midbrain or monkey brain, and finally your prefrontal cortex or sage brain. Your reptilian brain is the oldest part of your brain and is responsible for breathing, digestion, and circulation to name a few. All things that happen automatically to keep us alive, happen in the reptilian brain. We don't need to give these things any thought, our brain does them automatically. Your monkey brain is the part that chatters at you, warning you of danger that may or may not be real. Your sage brain is your thinking brain. Sometimes people call this the executive center of your brain. It is responsible for decision-making and creative thought.

It is your monkey brain that can cause the most problems for you when starting down the entrepreneurial path. There is a small almond-shaped gland in the center of your midbrain called the amygdala. It is responsible for the flight, fight, or freeze response. Neuroscientific studies have shown that negative thoughts trigger the brain's fear centers, impeding the rational thinking needed for effective communication and business promotion.

This neurological response not only affects the ability to articulate messages but also impedes the growth of coaching businesses. It's a pervasive force that whispers doubts about competence and worthiness, casting a shadow on the pursuit of goals. Recognizing and conquering this inner adversary is paramount for unlocking one's full potential.

YOUR INNER CRITIC

To unlock your fullest potential you will need to address and silence this inner adversary that lives in your monkey brain. I refer to this adversary as your inner critic. It is the little voice inside us that consistently says some not-so-nice things. Things like – who do you think you are? Why would anyone listen to what you have to say? You tried that before, what makes you think it will work this time? The litany of nasty grams from that inner critic is relentless. And the reason there is a constant stream of negativity is our inner critic thinks it is doing its job: keeping us safe. After all, if you never step foot on stage, speak up at a meeting, record a video and post it, or turn up at an event to meet new people, you'll stay safe and warm in your comfort zone. You will never get criticized, mocked, or laughed at. However, if you avoid leaving your comfort zone, you will never be able to grow your business or leave a legacy behind that will make a difference in the world.

The best course of action is to acknowledge this inner voice and work to move past it. This means befriending it. Understanding the role of your inner critic is to keep you safe. You can learn to harness the power of this voice and retrain your inner critic into an inner champion.

First, let's dig a bit deeper into the inner critic so we can begin to befriend it and rewire it for our benefit. Get out your journal and write down the answers to the following questions.

YOUR INNER CRITIC

What does it look like?

Where does it reside in your body?

What are some of the things it says to you on a regular basis?

Once you've written down your answers, sit with them for a few minutes. Please take the time to write your own. This is hard work. Congratulations for taking on this challenge. This work is foundational to the change you want to see in your life. Let me share my answers to these three questions to spark some inspiration.

MY EXAMPLE

1. *My inner critic is a little girl in a pink dress with pig tails, she looks a bit like Boo in the Disney movie Monsters, Inc. Her voice is nothing like Boo's, it is shrill and harsh and unpleasant.*
2. *She lives on my left shoulder where she can easily shout in my ear.*
3. *Who do you think you are? You've tried before and it didn't work, what is different this time? You are too old to start a business. You are not worthy or deserving of success. Nothing is as easy as you think it is going to be. What makes you so special? You really think people will pay you money? Give up now before you are a laughing stock.*

CHANGING YOUR INNER CRITIC

Be present with your inner critic so you can have a conversation that goes something like this:

Thank you so much for wanting to keep me safe. I know you want the best for me. Here's the deal, the way you are going about it isn't helpful. And I know you want to help. What I need in the future is for you to be supportive, and send me positive messages. I know you believe that if I put myself out there, I may get criticized. And that might happen, however, unless I give presentations and create videos no one will know how I can help them. No one will know about the amazing work I can do. So can we agree that going forward you will tell me things like – you are going to do a great job, your message is very important, people need to hear about what you do and how you can help them, you are going to be amazing, the audience will love you and what you have to say.

Work with your inner critic until it agrees it will try and help, it will change...eventually. Like anything worthwhile, it won't happen overnight. When speaking about this subject I often use a prop, a magic wand, and tell the audience I wish I had one to wave over them to magically silence the critic and bring forth the champion. There is no wand, no immediate change, it is the consistent application of new positive language that will change the critic to a champion. This will take some time and some work because no one, even the nasty little voice in our head, wants to be replaced. The neural pathways it has created are very deep. These pathways are similar to the ruts made by the wagon trains in the American West. For example, The Oregon Trail was used by people over 100 years ago and they are still visible today![1]

So let's create the champion. Begin by writing down the answers to these questions.

YOUR INNER CHAMPION
What does it look like?
Where does it reside in your body?
What are some of the things it says to you on a regular basis?

My inner champion looks like Wonder Woman (the one played by Linda Carter in the television series from 1975 to 1979.)

MY EXAMPLE

1. *Creating and running a business is a calling. One I cannot seem to let go of ...*
2. *My work is important because it make a difference in the lives of the clients I serve. I know this because they've told me. They've shared the success in their lives that came after we worked together...*
3. *My work makes a difference because it allows people to share their work in a powerful way in the world. The world needs to know about their work. As I often say, "you can't be the best kept secret in town and grow your business." When I help my clients overcome their fear of public speaking, getting on camera, or network to tell their story, it makes a positive impact in the world.*

She lives on my left shoulder, replacing my inner critic so she can shout in my ear.

And because I've worked to change the critical voice to one of encouragement each and every day, I take action to move forward and create the life and business of my dreams.

When I make a mistake or things don't go as planned tells me – she will say, "You are doing the best you can with the resources you have, you are learning and growing, and everyone starts somewhere the important thing is you started."

I've adopted Mel Robbins High 5 Habit. At the beginning of the day, when I look in the mirror, I give myself a high 5. My inner champion tells me how amazing I am. It says things like – you are doing great, look how far you've come, look at all the good you've produced, all the people you've helped. You keep going girl, there is no stopping you now!

Silencing the voice of your inner critic and bringing out the voice of your inner champion is foundational to success. That is why I start every session of my six-week Find Your Voice coaching program with a discussion about moving my student's inner critic to inner champion. If the only thing you do as the result of reading this book is the work required to quiet the critic and bring forth the champion, I will consider that a victory. I am not the only practitioner to encourage their followers to use positive internal language. Studying the work of Shad Helmstetter, Stephen R. Covey, Albert Ellis, Martin Seligman, and Shirzad Chamine have all influenced my life and my work. Let's take a few moments to review their work.

American Author Shad Helmstetter PhD

I first read Helmstetter's book, *What to Say When You Talk to Yourself* in the early 1990s. I found a copy at my local public library and was intrigued by the title. I discovered it not only explained why negative self-talk is the default, it contained a rich tapestry of language to put in its place. One of my first coaches was trained by Dr. Helmstetter himself who shepherded me down the path of befriending my inner critic and creating an inner champion. Here is a summary. Imagine your life as a room. When you are young the room is brand new. As you grow you create memories. These memories fill your room, like furniture. One of these pieces of furniture is your favorite sofa. Over time the sofa wears out and you decide to replace it. You carry it out the door to the back alley and leave it there. You try to fill your room with new furniture but it's just not as comfortable as that old sofa. So eventually you go back to the alley and drag that sofa back into your room. The sofa is part of your current mental program. It requires 3 things to change that programming.

1. Give new directions and messages to permanently rewire your brain.
2. Understand how your brain gets wired and your role in this wiring process.
3. Use specific positive vocabulary to override the old programming in your head.

Behavior, feelings, attitude, belief, and programming all work together to reprogram our critic into our inner champion. All input we receive is stored in our subconscious mind. Our critic and our champion live in our subconscious. The reality you desire is yours for the taking by changing the nasty negative voice to the critic into a positive powerful ally of a champion.

AMERICAN AUTHOR STEVEN R. COVEY

Covey's timeless classic *The 7 Habits of Highly Effective People* gives the reader 7 simple techniques to follow to build a life of influence and impact. The first three habits Covey calls private victories, be proactive, begin with the end in mind, and first things first are all habits we master within ourselves before moving on to public victory. Many people are attracted to the quick fix, the shiny object offering the easy way. He does a marvelous job of explaining why this won't work in the long run. We cannot circumvent the development process. Seeking shortcuts results in disappointment and frustration. "On a ten-point scale, if I am at level two in any field, and desire to move to level five. I must first take the step toward level three. 'A thousand-mile journey begins with the first step' and can only be taken one step at a time."

It was in Covey's book I first became aware of the idea of stimulus and response and that we always have a choice in how we respond to the events in our lives. He also introduced the concept of paying attention to the language we use in our minds as well as the words we speak.

For years, Liam felt like a prisoner in his mind. He was quick to react with anger and frustration, often blaming external circumstances for his feelings. Every event in Liam's life served as a stimulus (S), triggering an immediate response (R). He lacked the crucial space between the S and R, the gap where conscious choice resides. Instead, he felt like his emotions automatically pulled him towards negativity.

Liam also neglected the power of language. His

internal self-talk, riddled with negativity, fueled his pessimistic outlook. He'd often say, "Things will never change," reinforcing his feelings of helplessness.

One day, a friend introduced him to Covey's book. The idea of the "space between stimulus and response" resonated deeply. It was like being handed a bow and arrow, but realizing he was the one aiming, not the wind.

Liam began practicing mindfulness, paying attention to his thoughts and emotions without judgment. He started noticing the gap between events and his reactions. This space allowed him to choose a more conscious response, one informed by reason rather than automatic negativity.

He also actively changed his self-talk. He replaced phrases like "I can't" with "I will try." This shift in language empowered him to approach challenges with a more optimistic outlook.

The journey wasn't easy. But with consistent effort, Liam learned to become the archer, not the arrow. He developed the ability to control his reactions, manage his self-talk, and ultimately, shape his own experience

Liam's story demonstrates the power of awareness and conscious choice. By recognizing the space between stimulus and response and actively engaging with our self-talk, we can take control of our inner narrative and shape our responses to life's events in a more positive and empowering way.

AMERICAN PSYCHOLOGIST ALBERT ELLIS

Over the years I've taught many workshops to business professionals on stress management. In developing materials for these workshops I discovered the work of Psychologist Albert Ellis - Ellis focused on helping his clients understand the self-defeating ideas and irrational thoughts that contributed to maladaptive behavior. He sought to help participants reframe these thought patterns through a process called cognitive restructuring. Cognitive restructuring can be explained by one of the fundamental concepts of rational emotive behavior therapy (REBT) developed by Ellis—the ABC model. The ABC model proposes that the activating events (A) that occur in our lives cause us to develop beliefs (B) about those events that lead to emotional consequences (C).

Elias, a talented architect, was known for his innovative designs. However, a recent string of project rejections had left him feeling discouraged and unmotivated. He constantly berated himself, muttering, "I'm a failure. They'll never take me seriously." This self-deprecating narrative reflected the core of Albert Ellis's Rational Emotive Behavior Therapy (REBT) – the ABC model.

- **Activating Event (A):** Project rejections served as the activating event, triggering a series of internal reactions.

- **Beliefs (B):** Elias's interpretation of the rejections (B) was the crux of the issue. He held irrational beliefs such as, "My worth as an architect hinges on getting every project accepted." This inflated the importance of the rejections and fueled his negative emotions.
- **Consequences (C):** These irrational beliefs led to emotional consequences (C) like discouragement and self-doubt. The negativity paralyzed his creativity and motivation, hindering future projects.

One day, a mentor introduced Elias to the concept of REBT. The idea that his interpretations, not the events themselves, were driving his emotions resonated deeply. It was like being handed a new blueprint to navigate his career.

Elias began challenging his irrational beliefs. He reframed the rejections as opportunities for learning and improvement. "These rejections don't define me," he'd tell himself. "They're feedback to help me refine my work." He started focusing on the positive aspects – the skills he honed with each project, and the valuable feedback received.

This cognitive restructuring, a key component of REBT, empowered Elias. He started approaching his work with renewed enthusiasm. He focused on the creative process, the joy of design, and the journey of learning.

The outcome? Elias submitted a new project proposal, this time infused with his signature innovation and newfound confidence. This time, the response was positive. But even if it wasn't, Elias was prepared. He had learned to separate the activating events (project rejections) from his beliefs (self-worth not dependent on acceptance) and manage his emotional consequences (discouragement replaced with determination).

ACTION PLAN TO USE THE A+B=C FORMULA.

Now that we have had a chance to understand the formula, let's see how we can incorporate it into your mindset practice. Take a moment and draw out a table that looks like this:

Create **A** list of events in your life

Name your **B**elief about the event

Describe the **C**onsequences

In each section, write out your A's, B's, and C's. Next challenge that belief and change it to one that will serve you to take action to move forward into the life of your dreams.

To give you an idea of where to start, take a look at how I filled this table out:

A + B = C		
ACTIVATING EVENT	BELIEF	CONSEQUENCES
Failed speech contest	*I'm a terrible speaker*	*Kept me from improving my skills as a speaker*

For a long time, this belief stopped me from speaking up at work. It wasn't until I took a job where presenting to an audience was required that I did the work to change this belief.

MARTIN SELIGMAN FATHER OF POSITIVE PSYCHOLOGY

Seligman is often referred to as the father of positive psychology, the scientific study of human flourishing. His work has helped move psychology from a focus on pathology and illness to one of helping clients build upon their strengths and set goals to direct meaningful behavior.

Seligman first proposed that individuals have three

basic psychological needs:

- To feel positive emotion,
- Engage in activities that give life meaning and purpose, and
- Have positive relationships with others.

After more research and study, two other needs were subsequently added:

- Finding meaning and fulfillment in what we do and seek and
- Savoring achievements and accomplishments.

Seligman's PERMA model which stands for **P**ositive Emotions, **E**ngagement, **R**elationships, **M**eaning, and **A**chievement has been expanded to include **H**ealth. Now known as PERMAH I came across his work when I was developing a program for a business client and immediately became a fan of his science-based exercises to enhance my wellbeing.

Ever since childhood, Maya had dreamt of becoming a renowned artist, her heart yearning to express vibrant emotions on canvas. However, life had thrown its fair share of challenges, leaving her feeling unmotivated and disconnected. This disconnect manifested in the form of a constant internal tug-of-war, mirroring the elements of Seligman's PERMA model.

Negative Emotions: The negativity surrounding her

unfulfilled dream bled into other areas. Simple tasks felt overwhelming, and joy seemed a distant memory.

Disengagement: Engaging in her art, once a source of immense pleasure, now felt like a chore. Inspiration had faded, replaced by a sense of apathy.

Strained Relationships: The emotional toll impacted her relationships. The spark in her interactions with friends and family dimmed, creating a sense of isolation.

Lack of Meaning: Maya questioned the purpose behind her struggles. The absence of fulfillment in her art career spilled over, casting a shadow on her overall sense of meaning.

Limited Achievements: The demotivation further hindered her artistic journey. The lack of progress in her art fueled her self-doubt, creating a vicious cycle.

Declining Health: The emotional turmoil affected her physical well-being. Sleep became erratic, and healthy habits were neglected, further exacerbating her emotional state.

Desperate for a change, Maya stumbled upon Martin Seligman's work and the PERMAH model. The framework resonated with her, offering a roadmap to reclaiming well-being. This encounter, like finding a forgotten paintbrush, sparked a renewed sense of agency.

Positive Emotions: Maya started practicing gratitude exercises, focusing on the little joys in life. She reconnected with activities that brought her simple pleasures, like walks in nature and listening to uplifting music. Slowly, a smile returned to her face.

Engagement: With renewed positive emotions, Maya started taking small steps toward her artistic passion. She joined online art communities, seeking inspiration and engaging with other artists. The act of creation, fueled by positive emotions, brought back the joy of art.

Strengthened Relationships: Engaging with the art community fostered new connections and rekindled existing ones. Sharing her art with others and receiving positive feedback fostered a sense of belonging and support.

Finding Meaning: As Maya reconnected with her passion and actively engaged in her art, she discovered a renewed sense of purpose. She realized that the journey itself held meaning, not just the destination of achieving fame.

Achievements: With consistent effort and newfound engagement, Maya started seeing progress in her art. Each completed piece, each new skill learned, became a small achievement, fueling her motivation and propelling her forward.

Improved Health: As Maya addressed the various aspects of her well-being, a positive ripple effect emerged. Improved sleep, healthier eating habits, and regular exercise contributed to her overall physical health, further bolstering her emotional and creative drive.

Maya's journey illustrates how neglecting any

element of PERMAH can create an imbalance, impacting overall well-being. However, by consciously addressing each element, we can cultivate a vibrant and fulfilling life, just like an artist painting a masterpiece with a diverse and rich palette.

SHIRZAD CHAMINE LIFE COACH AND AUTHOR

It was only recently I became acquainted with the work of Shirzad Chamine, creator of Positive Intelligence. My own coach is certified in this work, which can only be described as breakthrough research. It identified the core factors that impact both performance and well-being, revealing that there are only 10 negative response factors (10 Saboteurs) and only five positive response factors (5 Sage Powers). Locating we rewire our brain at the root level rather than treating symptoms. Stopping one's Saboteur and calling upon one's Sage automatically results in a variety of impacts including stress management, relationship improvement, performance, selling and persuasion, creativity, leadership, resilience, and happiness.

Imagine, if you will, Anya, a gifted weaver, who had always dreamed of showcasing her intricate tapestries at the annual Autumn Fair. But a persistent voice, a familiar echo in her mind, always held her back. "Your work isn't good enough," it would hiss. "They'll laugh at you." This relentless negativity, Anya later learned, was her "Saboteur," a term coined by Shirzad Chamine in his book Positive Intelligence.

Desperate to break free from this internal critic, Anya embarked on a journey to the Whispering Canyon. Legend spoke of a wise woman, the "Mystic," residing there, who possessed the power to silence inner saboteurs. After weeks of arduous travel, Anya found the Sage meditating in a hidden cave.

Anya poured her heart out, explaining her dream and the voice that stifled it. The Mystic, with eyes that held the wisdom of ages, smiled gently. "Anya," she said, "we all have voices within us, one that whispers fear and doubt, the other that speaks of courage and potential. You cannot erase the Saboteur, but you can choose to amplify the voice of your inner Champion."

The Mystic then gifted Anya a small, woven pendant with a single, shimmering thread. "This," she explained, "represents your positive voice. Each time the Saboteur speaks, weave a new thread into the pendant. With every act of self-compassion, every step towards your dream, your Sage will grow stronger."

Anya hugged the pendant close to her heart. Returning home, she started small. Instead of focusing on the negative, she celebrated her progress, each completed stitch a victory. She joined a weaving circle, sharing her work and receiving positive feedback. With each new thread woven into the pendant, Anya's confidence blossomed.

Finally, the Autumn Fair arrived. Anya, nervous yet

determined, unveiled her masterpiece tapestry. People were awestruck by its beauty. The once-whispering voice was now a distant echo, overpowered by the symphony of compliments and the quiet pride within Anya. She had replaced her Saboteur with a Sage, woven from self-belief and positive action.

Consider using a talisman, as Anya did, when you need to draw near to your champion and silence the inner critic.

I offer all of this to say what I've come to believe. Positive self-talk is a powerful tool for reshaping our thinking. It influences how we interpret situations and view ourselves, ultimately shaping our emotions, behavior, and overall well-being.

One of my favorite authors is James Clear and his book *Atomic Habits*. After reading his book I signed up to receive his weekly email newsletter and in one issue he said, "You do not rise to the level of your goals. You fall to the level of your systems." This idea resonated with me. We are all well-intended when we set down the path to success. Yet, life can get in the way unless we have systems in place to keep us moving forward. Based on his quote my question to you today is - what systems have you put in place to summon your inner champion and silence your inner critic? You need systems, maybe you prefer the word routine or ritual. It is not what you call it that is important. What is important is that you have a method to get back on track when you get derailed. It is the old analogy that when life throws you lemons, make lemonade. What is your system to create lemonade? As the Japanese proverb reminds us - *fall down 7 times, stand up 8*.

I have a few systems in my life. One is my morning routine. I developed a routine that includes meditation, yoga, and my gratitude journal. I've modeled after what Tony Robbins calls Power Hour, the first 60 minutes when you awake each day. I didn't always start my day in such a fashion. In my twenties, I sleep as late as possible and rush around to get out the door. At that time I carpooled to work and my friend, who drove, would often wait in my driveway for 5 or more minutes. Until one day she said, if you can't be ready when I arrive, I'm not going to pick you up anymore. I got the message and changed my ways.

When we win the morning, we win the day. If you don't already have a morning routine that sets your day up for success, I encourage you to create one.

Another maximum I would encourage you to adopt is to get comfortable with being uncomfortable. Do one thing every day that scares you. It doesn't have to be a big thing, maybe it is picking up the phone and calling a past customer or attending a networking event. As businessman Dave Morin reminds us, we must act now because uncomfortable things get harder the longer we wait.

Create an alter ego to call on when you need it. Did you know Beyonce has Sasha Fierce? Sasha comes out when she puts on her stilettos and walks on stage.

Bring out yours before you step in front of a group to deliver a talk, lead a meeting, or hit record and create a video. Just like Beyonce, give it a name (Sasha Fierce) and create a trigger (putting on her stilettos). Look at this technique as another way to call on your inner champion.

The other idea was in a podcast I listened to a few months ago. I do not recall the name of the podcast, or the guest being interviewed, that's not what is important. What is important is the guest was talking about imposter syndrome, something many of us face. She calls her alter ego Kevin and when it acts up and starts the trash talk inside her head, she exclaims out loud "Not Today Kevin, Not Today!"

Stepping out and speaking up is hard work, that is why an inner champion, a voice of encouragement, a voice that says you've got this, a voice that says helps you move forward is so important. Please avoid letting your inner critic stop you from taking action. Every gold medal winner I've ever read about had a pre-game routine. An example of this is Michael Phelps his routine before every race was the same. By doing the same thing every time there was no room for stress or worry.

STRATEGIES TO SUMMON YOUR INNER CHAMPION.

Affirmations

The words we choose to say about ourselves have power. The language we use predicts triumph or tragedy. What comes out of your mouth comes into your life. Create a list of positive affirmations from your inner champion. Affirmations start with the words "I am" and use positive powerful language. Examples include: I am a confident and powerful presenter. I am focused and productive every day. I am amazing. I am a strong, capable person. I am proud of myself and will continue to strive to do well. Create a list of at least 10 affirmations to speak out loud, with enthusiasm twice a day, once at the beginning and once at the end.

A Garden of Support

Picture yourself in a garden of beautiful plants and flowers. It is a warm, wonderful place of quiet solitude. The plants in this garden are different from other plants in the world. Instead of taking in oxygen and giving off CO2, these plants give off calm and relaxation while taking in your stress. You breathe out stress and anxiety and breathe in the calming fragrance of the plants in this garden. You can return to this garden any time of day, anytime you need to recenter yourself and recharge. Couple this with the following idea on breathing.

Use Your Breathe to Refocus

When your inner critic is shouting in your ear, stop

and take 5 deep breaths. Inhaling to the count of 4, holding your inhale for 4 counts, exhaling for the count of 4, and holding your exhale for 4 counts. This technique can help calm your central nervous system and help you improve your performance and concentration.

Use Your 5 Senses

Change your focus by noticing 5 things you can see, 4 things you can touch, 3 things you can hear, 2 things you can smell, and 1 thing you can taste. Intentionally shifting your focus can calm your central nervous system and get you to take action.

Ask What If?

When we get anxious or worried, we don't even realize how often we are "What if - ing"... Say I'm planning an outdoor wedding and as it gets closer, my anxiety mounts around the weather....., "What if it rains??!!" And I never answer that question... "What if it DOES rain? What will I do"

When I picture what I will do if it does rain, I'm better able to come up with a solution. Rent a tent, have indoor space available as an alternative, etc. When I picture it, and I picture the solution, and I picture myself handling the solution, my anxiety subsides. Even if I don't LOVE the solution, at least I can picture surviving it.

The exercise goes like this:

What If...

1. *"What if ______________________________ " "I lose my job, ... I don't get the promotion, ... my kid flunks geometry....... my baby is born with a handicap....*
2. **Now you need to picture it... picture the thing in the "what if" actually happening.**
3. *"What will I do if______________________. What if people ridicule my presentation?*
4. **Picture it, picture how you will handle it, what support mechanisms you will use?**
5. **Finally, and this is the most important part...**
6. *"How likely is it that _______________ will happen?"*

Most of the time the things that are making us the most anxious, are not highly likely.

I want to thank my colleague Mary Jo Baweja of Blank Canvas Consulting for sharing this idea with me. It is one she uses with her clients.

CONCLUSION

The stories we carry in our minds possess the remarkable ability to either halt our progress or propel us forward on the path to success. Perhaps, up until now, the presence of your inner critic has operated in the shadows, subtly influencing the trajectory of your life. It's time to shed light on this internal narrative and take intentional steps to befriend it. By understanding and leveraging your inner critic positively and powerfully, you can transform it from a potential hindrance into a driving force for personal and professional growth. Remember, inspiration and resilience are not exclusive to the rich and famous. Consider the ordinary individual next door, navigating life's challenges with grace and determination. Their story, filled with everyday triumphs, serves as a testament to the transformative power of embracing and redirecting our inner dialogue. As you continue your journey, recognize that within your narrative lies the potential for extraordinary achievement.

CHAPTER 5

CAMERA CONFIDENCE: MASTERING THE ART OF ON-CAMERA STORYTELLING FOR VIDEO MARKETING

> "Photography is a way of feeling, of touching, of loving. What you have caught on film is captured forever… It remembers little things, long after you have forgotten everything."— Aaron Siskind

The ubiquitous smartphone has made it so easy for everyone to record and post video content. The camera lens can be both a formidable adversary and a steadfast ally, influencing how your message resonates with your audience. We will start by disclosing what makes us reluctant to create video content and how to get comfortable in front of the camera. I will share pointers on audience engagement through storytelling, exploring not only the nuances of body language but also how to create a commanding stage presence that comes across authentically. Everyone has a unique personality, let yours shine through. The overall goal of any presentation using a camera is to take your business to the next level. Engaging with a larger and larger audience. Mastering the art of on-camera storytelling is not just about facing the lens; it's a blend of sharing your moments of weakness and strength. As a business owner, you're not just telling a story – you're crafting an experience that goes beyond pixels and resonates with genuineness, creating a lasting relationship with your audience. Embrace the camera, for within its frame lies the gateway to true connection and business elevation.

UNDERSTANDING THE LENS

While mastering the technical aspects of video recording is important, truly captivating on-camera storytelling reaches deeper into the fascinating realm of communication psychology. The camera goes beyond being a mere recording device; it becomes a powerful conduit for transmitting emotions, genuineness, and a sense of connection.

Stepping on camera isn't just about physical presence; it's about journeying into the minds and hearts of your audience. The key to an effective on-camera presence lies in your ability to come across authentically. Your audience isn't just there for information, they yearn for genuine connections. When you stand before the lens with sincerity, vulnerability, and a profound understanding of your message, you bridge the gap between the virtual and the personal, fostering a deeper connection.

Understanding the psychological impact of being on camera allows us to acknowledge and address the common fears and anxieties associated with creating video content. Fears of judgment, the "imposter syndrome," and the pressure to perform flawlessly can impede authentic self-expression. In the next few paragraphs, we will discuss these one by one. Allowing you to explore the on-camera experience with confidence, authenticity, and a newfound appreciation for its potential. It is not just about being seen, but truly connecting with those watching your message unfold.

FEAR OF JUDGMENT

One of the most pervasive challenges individuals face when embracing on-camera presence is the deeply rooted fear of judgment. This fear often stems from the exposure inherent in putting oneself in the public eye.

The fear of judgment can manifest in various ways. People may worry about their appearance, the way they articulate ideas, or whether their message will resonate with the audience. This fear is closely linked to the desire for validation and acceptance, as individuals expose not just their expertise but also a part of themselves when they step into the limelight.

It's essential to recognize that this fear is not a sign of

weakness but a universal human experience. Acknowledging and normalizing this fear creates a foundation for growth. Encouraging self-compassion and emphasizing that perfection is not the goal allows individuals to shift their focus from seeking approval to delivering value and authenticity. Remember it is about the pursuit of excellence, not perfection. Take a look at the early work of any "influencer" you follow on social media and notice the difference time has made in their work.

One method of conquering the fear of judgment lies in a shift in perspective. Instead of imagining the audience as a panel of critics, see them as enthusiastic learners eager for your valuable insights. This reframing fosters a mindset focused on knowledge sharing and connection, replacing fear with the excitement of meaningful engagement and personal growth. By approaching the camera as a platform for positive interaction, individuals can transform their on-camera experience.

The goal is to step into the camera's gaze with confidence, knowing that your authenticity is the true currency in the world of on-camera storytelling.

IMPOSTER-SYNDROME

Imposter syndrome can be a formidable adversary. It can feel like a shadow looming over us, filling your mind with doubt about your expertise and accomplishments. At its core, imposter syndrome shows up as an internalized belief that despite external evidence of competence, one is an imposter or fraud. When you step in front of the camera to share your insights and experiences, it whispers doubts about whether you truly deserve to be in the spotlight. If you listen to these falsehoods, it can undermine confidence, authenticity, and the ability to effectively communicate your message. We spent a great deal of time in the last chapter developing your inner champion. It is a powerful tool to defeat this internal voice of sabotage.

In addition, Imposter syndrome often thrives in the shadows of isolation, so fostering a community where individuals can openly share their insecurities and receive support is pivotal.

Another way this foe can be tackled is by reframing success as a journey, not a destination. Accepting that growth is an ongoing process fueled by learning and growth. This shift will allow you to embrace your expertise and confidently share your knowledge.

Are you familiar with the term confirmation bias? This is when your brain looks for evidence to confirm or support your belief. Avoid confirming you are not capable or knowledgeable by incorporating one or all of the following ideas to counterbalance negative confirmation bias. Make it a practice to ask for feedback once someone has completed their sessions or program with you. Create a file, either digital or paper, where you store this collection of positive comments on your work and the impact you have made in the lives of your clients. You can pull these out and refer to them when the voices of doubt shout in your ear. I recall reading an article from a successful author who posted fan mail on the wall above his writing desk so he could refer to the notes when he needed to be reassured of his worthiness.

Start a "It Is Finished List" by writing down 3 actions you took to build your business at the end of each day. This will enable you to look back in time and see how much you've accomplished.

Talk to yourself like your best friend would. Consider writing down the answer to this question - what would my best friend tell me to encourage me to continue to take action?

Take action. In a conversation with my coach recently, I said, "I think what I need is a pep talk", instead of that she gave me an assignment. A specific action I could take to build my business. When you are taking action there is no time to dwell on the negative.

PRESSURE TO PERFORM

The pressure to perform can stem from various sources – the desire for perfection, the fear of making mistakes, or the anticipation of meeting external standards. Coaches, in their role as guides and mentors, may feel a heightened responsibility to exemplify the very principles they advocate for their clients. This expectation, while aspirational, can become a source of stress and hinder the authentic expression of one's message.

The on-camera journey is not a solo performance but a collaborative dialogue. Shift your focus from delivering a flawless presentation to engaging in a meaningful conversation with your audience. Embracing imperfections, acknowledging that mistakes are part of the learning process, and allowing authenticity to shine through are powerful antidotes to the pressure to perform.

My first attempts at creating video content involved hours of re-recording: spending several 4-hour sessions on some Saturday mornings to create one 6-minute YouTube video. I finally decided that done was better than perfect. Now before I get on camera, I do one run-through of my material out loud, hit record, and then upload it to my editing software. This is now a 20-to-30-minute process.

Furthermore, setting realistic expectations and emphasizing the value of the message over the pursuit of perfection can redefine success in on-camera presence. Encouraging a mindset that views each on-camera interaction as an opportunity for growth, connection, and learning helps dissipate the pressure to perform.

START WITH A POWERFUL OPENING

Now let's shift our focus (pun intended) to uncover the impact of visual storytelling on audience engagement. The start and the finish of your video are your guideposts and will help you fill in the middle.

Attention spans are getting shorter and shorter these days. In the never-ending scroll through social media, it is hard to predict what makes people stop and listen or what makes a video turn viral. Avoid creating videos for those two reasons. Create a story that will resonate with and attract your ideal client. Don't be afraid to give away your best advice, tips, or tricks. Share without hesitation. When someone sees your video, you want them to think; "Hey, this person gets me!" That way they are more likely to follow, like, and share. The initial goal is to connect.

The first seven to ten words out of your mouth need to be compelling and engaging. Avoid starting with pleasantries like "Hello Friends" or "In today's video I will share…" I've been guilty of both. My top-performing video today starts with the words; "There are three philosophies that I like." Make a provocative statement based on your niche such as:

- Health coaches - "Feeling tired and stressed is the new 'normal.' But it doesn't have to be."
- Financial coaches - "You don't need a six-figure income to retire comfortably."
- Women's life coaches - "You're done playing by everyone else's rules. It's time to design a life YOU love."
- Business coaches - "Your biggest competitor isn't who you think it is. It's your outdated business model."

- Marriage coaches - "Your 'happily ever after' doesn't have to be a fairy tale. It can be a thrilling adventure – together."

Grab your audience's attention from the start. When I was a kid, I recall a cliché often used to parody a poor method of opening a novel was – "It was a dark and stormy night." The same is true of the opening line in your video. Research indicates the average adult's attention span is just 8 seconds. The first words out of your mouth must be designed to engage with your target audience. Otherwise, they are scrolling away from you and on to the next item in their social media feed. There are any number of ways you can start a video that will grab your target audience's attention. Consider the following:

- **Present a relatable scenario**: Start by painting a picture of a situation your ideal client might be facing. This could be a brief anecdote, a relatable story, or even a humorous skit. For example, a productivity coach might open with a scene of someone frantically searching for their keys while rushing out the door.
- **Ask a captivating question:** Pose a question that taps into a common pain point or desire of your target audience. This instantly engages them and makes them curious about

the answer you'll provide later in the video. For example, a career coach might ask: "Feeling stuck in a job that doesn't fulfill you? You're not alone. But what if you could find work you love?"

- **Share a surprising statistic:** Hook viewers with a data point or statistic relevant to your niche. This grabs your attention and establishes you as an expert with valuable insights. A life coach targeting busy professionals might open with: "Did you know that chronic stress can decrease your productivity by 20%?"
- **Show a problem in action:** Visually demonstrate a common challenge your audience faces. This could be a short screen recording of a cluttered inbox for a time management coach or a montage of people looking exhausted for a sleep coach.
- **Start with a powerful testimonial:** Showcase the positive impact you've had on a previous client. Hearing a success story from someone similar to them instantly builds trust and credibility for your coaching services.

The best opening grabs attention quickly, sparks an emotional response, and effectively sets the stage for the rest of your video content.

END WITH A LASTING IMPRESSION

Once you have your opening, create the ending. A strong ending should summarize the major takeaways, leave viewers feeling empowered, and provide a clear path for them to take action or learn more. Imagine building a wall around your content. The opening and closing statements are the border that creates a connection. The following five ways will wrap up a video to leave a lasting impression and encourage viewers to take action:

Call to action (CTA) with a deadline: End with a clear and specific call to action and add a sense of urgency with a deadline. This could be a free consultation offer that expires in 48 hours, a discount code valid for one week, or early bird pricing for an upcoming workshop. One recent virtual workshop I attended gave a significant discount on the program if the purchase was made by midnight that day.

Empowering statement and next steps: Leave viewers feeling motivated and empowered to take the next step. Briefly summarize your key message and provide actionable steps they can implement right away. For example, a confidence coach might end with: "Remember, you are capable of achieving anything you set your mind to. Start by identifying one small action you can take today to boost your confidence."

Compelling question and community invitation: End with a thought-provoking question that lingers with viewers after the video ends. This encourages reflection and keeps them engaged. Additionally, invite them to join your online community, such as a Facebook group or email list, for ongoing support and resources. A health coach might end a video in this way: "Alright, that's all the time I have for today. But I want to leave you with this: are you truly prioritizing your health amidst the daily hustle? Remember, you can't pour from an empty cup. What's one small change you can commit to today to invest in your well-being?"

Teaser for future content: End with a sneak peek at what's coming next. This could be a teaser for another video series, a free downloadable guide, or an upcoming workshop. Spark their interest and encourage them to subscribe for more valuable content. You often see this on television describing what will be presented in the upcoming evening news or weather segments. The local weather person comes on screen to say "Storms could bring heavy winds and rain, details at 11".

Storytelling with a cliffhanger: If your video uses storytelling as a core element, consider ending with a cliffhanger. Briefly share a personal anecdote or client success story and leave a key detail unresolved. This piques their curiosity and motivates them to seek out the full story, perhaps through your website or social media.

Here's an example of a cliffhanger ending for a life coach targeting women between 45 and 60:

(Appear on the screen, looking thoughtful) "I used to feel stuck like I was going through the motions of life without any real purpose. My days were filled with obligations, but there was a hollowness inside. Then, I stumbled upon a simple journaling exercise that completely transformed my perspective..."

(Screen fades to black with text overlay: "Want to know the journaling exercise that reignited my passion? Subscribe for the next video!")

The best ending should feel complete and satisfying while also encouraging viewers to take the next step in their coaching journey.

Think of this method of crafting an opening statement then your closing statement like solving a jigsaw puzzle. Most puzzle solvers I know start by sorting out the pieces that create the outside border first. These edge pieces provide the frame for the entire image. They give you context for what the bigger picture will be. Once you have the border secured, you can move on to filling in the rest of the pieces, those intricate details that bring the story to life.

It's the same with crafting a story. Your opening should be like those edge pieces. It grabs your audience's attention, introduces the main characters and the central conflict, and establishes the setting. It primes your listeners for the journey ahead. Then, just like the satisfying click of a puzzle piece slotting into place, your closing should bring everything together. It should tie up any loose ends, reinforce your main themes, and leave your audience with a lasting impression. A strong opening and closing are the cornerstones of any effective story.

ALIGN YOUR VIDEO CONTENT WITH YOUR BRAND MESSAGE

Your video content is a powerful tool for connecting with your audience and establishing your brand identity. But simply creating videos isn't enough. To truly connect with viewers, your video content needs to be strategically aligned with your core brand message. This means ensuring that every visual element, from the editing style to the language used, reflects the values, personality, and mission of your brand.

Think of your brand message as the heart of your video content. It's the central theme that should weave its way throughout every piece you create. Are you known for being informative and educational? Fun and lighthearted? Authoritative and trustworthy? Let your brand message guide your video content decisions. For example, if your brand prioritizes approachability, you might opt for a casual and conversational tone in your videos. If expertise is your key strength, your videos might incorporate data visualizations and feature interviews with industry leaders. By ensuring this alignment, you create a cohesive and memorable brand experience for your viewers. They do a great job connecting their brand message to the content they create.

I don't know about you, but I often get inspiration from others who are leading the way. You may have people you follow because their message resonates with you. I offer them as examples because I've enjoyed their content, and they may spark an idea or two for you.

Marie Kondo (Lifestyle Organization):

Marie Kondo, the queen of tidying up, uses her YouTube channel and other social media platforms to perfectly embody her brand message of "sparking joy." Her videos feature calming visuals of decluttering spaces, soothing music, and her gentle guidance. She avoids sensationalizing the process and instead focuses on the peace and well-being achieved through organization. This consistency between her brand message (sparking joy) and the visual and emotional tone of her videos creates a strong and recognizable brand identity.

Mark Rober (Science Communication):

Mark Rober, a former NASA engineer turned YouTuber, uses humor, engaging experiments, and high-quality production value to communicate complex scientific concepts. His brand message is clear: science can be fun, informative, and entertaining. His videos never shy away from the "science" part, but they do so in a way that is visually stimulating and uses humor to keep viewers engaged. This alignment between his brand message (fun and engaging science) and the content and style of his videos makes him a popular science communicator.

Zach King (Illusionist/Content Creator):

Zach King's videos are like magic tricks come to life. His brand message is being the master of mind-bending illusions and creativity. Zach uses clever editing techniques, special effects, and creative storytelling to create mind-boggling illusions that defy reality. The humor and surprise in his videos keep viewers engaged and wanting more. This alignment makes him a master of the unexpected and a pioneer in the illusionist content creator space.

Dr. Jessica Garner (Dermatologist/Skincare Expert):

Dr. Garner's videos feature a relaxed and informative approach. Her brand message embodies a trustworthy and down-to-earth dermatologist providing science-backed skincare advice. She debunks skincare myths, explains the science behind ingredients, and offers practical tips for viewers to achieve healthy skin. The casual yet professional tone makes her approachable and relatable, while the scientific backing positions her as a credible expert. This consistency builds trust and positions her as a go-to source for reliable skincare information.

Marie Forleo (Business Coach/Entrepreneur):

Marie Forleo's videos are high-energy and motivational. Marie's message is empowering women entrepreneurs to build successful and fulfilling businesses. She shares actionable business tips, interviews successful entrepreneurs, and encourages viewers to take action toward their goals. The positive and encouraging tone reflects her brand message of empowerment, while the practical advice positions her as a valuable resource for aspiring businesswomen. This alignment inspires and equips viewers to pursue their entrepreneurial dreams.

By creating content that reflects their core message, these influencers establish strong brand identities and cultivate loyal followings. They understand that video content is a powerful tool not just for entertainment, but for building trust, credibility, and a lasting connection with their audience.

OWNING YOUR SPACE: BODY LANGUAGE TIPS FOR CONFIDENCE ON CAMERA

Body language plays a crucial role in how you come across on camera, especially when it comes to projecting confidence. Let's explore some practical tips to help you convey conviction through posture, gestures, and facial expressions, while also addressing common pitfalls and maintaining authenticity.

PROJECTING CONFIDENCE:

Posture: Sit or stand tall with your shoulders back and relaxed, core engaged, feet flat on the floor. Imagine a string pulling you up from the crown of your head. This posture exudes power and presence. Remove pens, rubber bands, and paper clips from your hands so you won't be tempted to fidget with them. Fidgeting, slouching, hunching all convey nervousness.

Slouching compresses your lungs, and you won't be able to breathe as deeply. Shallow breaths can add to your nervous state. I have a post-it note above my camera where I record my YouTube content reminding me to keep my feet on the floor, sit up straight and breathe deeply.

Gestures: Use natural hand gestures to emphasize your points but avoid excessive or distracting movements. Most of the time have your hands comfortably by your side if you are standing or on your lap if you are seated. Open palms facing the camera are inviting, while closed fists can come across as aggressive.

Put down pens or markers to avoid leaving an accidental mark across your face. Years before self-made video content was available my boss delivered a presentation using a flip chart and marker. At the break she went into the ladies' room, looked in the mirror and realized to her horror she had swiped the black marker across her face giving herself a mustache. No one in the audience had said a word about it.

Facial Expressions: Maintain eye contact with the camera lens. Imagine you are speaking with your best friend. This will help you appear as if you are making eye contact with the viewer. Nothing will lose an audience quicker than failing to make eye contact. You want to create a connection and be more engaging. Before you hit the button to record, smile. You don't need a big toothy grin, use a genuine smile at the beginning and end of your video. In the middle let your natural facial expressions reflect your enthusiasm for the topic.

The more I attend virtual meetings the more I notice how many people fail to position their camera so that they are looking directly into the eyes of their fellow participants. Make sure your video camera lines up with your eyes. It wasn't until my coach viewed some of my videos on social media that I realized I was making this mistake. I was looking down into the camera instead of lining it up with my direct gaze.

COMMON PITFALLS AND HOW TO AVOID THEM:

Stepping in front of a camera can evoke a myriad of emotions, from exhilaration to paralyzing fear. Despite knowing it is important to leverage the power of video to connect with our audience and promote our services; we often find ourselves grappling with subconscious behaviors that sabotage our on-camera presence. When faced with heightened anxiety we can manifest behaviors that subconsciously help us keep calm. However these behaviors disconnect us from our audience, making us look unsure instead of confident. I uncovered a couple of my own idiosyncrasies when I began using a software program for closed captioning for my YouTube channel videos.

The Nervous Tic: We all have them - hair twirling, foot tapping, biting your lip, etc. View a few recordings of yourself to see what you need to stop. Be mindful of these habits and try to replace them with more confident gestures. Take a few long slow deep breaths before filming to calm your nerves. It was not until I started adding closed captions on my videos that I noticed how often I started sentences with the word "so" and said "wanna" instead of want to.

The Paced Walker: If you find yourself pacing back and forth, consider using a standing desk or marking a designated spot on the floor to keep your movement contained. When you move, move with purpose. Lean in when making an important point. Shift back when you are ending the story. Even 'famous' people make this mistake. I viewed an online event hosted by an actor reinventing himself as a motivational speaker. His constant pacing forward and backward was distracting from the valuable message he shared during the event. You'd have thought someone from Hollywood might not have made that mistake.

The Downward Gaze: Looking down at notes or the floor breaks eye contact and weakens your presence. If you need reference points, use cue cards strategically placed near the camera. No one except you can see what is behind the camera. Create a setup that allows you to look directly into the camera lens giving the impression you are looking into the eyes of the audience.

Consider placing a whiteboard or a cork board behind your camera so you can refer to notes and avoid looking down. Sticky notes work for this purpose, too.

The Robot: Stiff and unmoving body language can be off-putting. Remember, some natural movement is okay, it shows you're comfortable and engaged. Before hitting the record button put on your favorite dance music and move. This will allow you to shake out your body to loosen up your joints.

Be Yourself: When you show up on camera in a genuine way, you build trust and connection with your audience, as they can sense your sincerity and authenticity. Being yourself means embracing your quirks, imperfections, and peculiarities. It's about having the courage to be vulnerable and share your authentic story, knowing that it's through our openness that we truly connect with others. By embracing authenticity, you invite others to do the same, creating a space where genuine connections can flourish.

Moreover, being yourself is empowering. It frees you from the pressure of trying to conform to societal norms or meet unrealistic expectations. Instead, it allows you to celebrate your uniqueness and share your perspective with the world. When you embrace authenticity, you give yourself permission to be unapologetically you, and that is where your true power lies.

Avoid Mimicking Others: Spend some time viewing influencers on the social media platform you use as reference. While it's helpful to learn from other confident presenters, avoid copying their mannerisms exactly. Find what feels natural and comfortable for you. My husband is my biggest supporter and critic. He is not mean spirited; he simply points out how I'm coming across in the video. In a couple of cases I've removed the post because he was right, it made me look bad.

Embrace Your Personality: Let your unique personality shine through. Your passion and enthusiasm for your topic will naturally come across as confidence. Tony Robbins is passionate about his work. You can see that any time he is on camera. John Maxwell is passionate about his work with a totally different communication style. Compare and contrast the video content of two popular female YouTube coaches Lisa Bilyeu and Aileen Xu.

Practice Makes Progress: The more you record yourself on camera, the more comfortable you'll become. Record practice sessions and review them to see what works and what you can improve on.

Becoming confident on camera takes practice. When you're focused on delivering valuable content, your confidence will naturally shine through. Use these tips and stay true to yourself. You can develop a powerful and authentic on-camera presence that resonates with your audience.

CHARISMATIC CONFIDENCE WILL COMMAND ATTENTION

Imagine facing a camera with unwavering confidence, effortlessly captivating your audience with every word you speak. What if I told you that charisma and commanding attention are not innate qualities reserved for the lucky few, but skills that can be honed and mastered by anyone? In this section, we dive into the art of enhancing charisma and commanding attention, equipping you with practical exercises and techniques to elevate your presence and leave a lasting impact in any self-promotion scenario. Incorporate the following exercises to create a routine before you hit the record button. Remember the actions of confidence come before the feelings of confidence.

Power Pose Practice: Stand tall, with your feet shoulder-width apart, hands on hips or raised triumphantly overhead. This posture not only boosts confidence but also conveys authority and presence. I've taken to heart Harvard professor Amy Cuddy's advice, practicing what she refers to as the Wonder Woman pose before I hit the record button or step out on stage. It helps me become grounded and focused.

Mirror Work: Practice speaking in front of a mirror to observe their body language, facial expressions, and vocal tone. Play with a variety of gestures, smiles, and eye contact. Very few people like this work, my clients often moan and groan when I suggest it. Yet it is one of the most powerful ways to enhance your confidence and connection with the audience. Don't like the mirror? Use your smartphone and create a recording you can delete after you've reviewed it for your own evaluation.

Voice Modulation Exercises: Several years ago I joined 15 other speakers at an event to create video content to be used as a "sizzle reel", used to send meeting planners to get hired for an event. I was new to the speaking world and was astonished at how many of the seasoned experts spent time warming up their vocal cords making sounds that increased and decreased in volume and tone. Practice voice modulation exercises by experimenting with pitch, pace, volume, and intonation to convey emotion, emphasis, and authority. This will help you vary your speaking style to keep the audience engaged and attentive.

Presence Practice: Incorporate mindfulness techniques to cultivate presence and focus before stepping on camera. Use deep breathing, visualization, and grounding exercises to calm nerves and center yourself in the present moment. Genuine presence is magnetic and will naturally draw attention and respect from others. There are several ideas at the end of chapter 4.

FINALLY LET'S TALK TECH

The chapter would not be complete without a word about how to set up your camera, along with a variety of tech tools to support your efforts so you look great in front of your viewers.

Center yourself within the frame of the camera. When your webcam is the height where you are looking directly into it, this will allow you to be in the center of the frame. When your webcam is too high, you appear to be looking up and when it's too low you appear to be looking down. This was a rookie mistake I made until both my coach and my husband commented I was looking down in my video instead of holding the gaze of my audience. Be sure to position your webcam or your smartphone so that you are looking into your own eyes, this will project to looking into the eyes of your viewer.

You've heard the phrase lights, camera, action. There is a reason lights come first. You need to be well-lit so people can see your face. Again another novice mistake I made until someone who viewed my first YouTube videos brought it to my attention. It doesn't have to be expensive either. I recently purchased two 60 LED tabletop photography lights that sit on either side of my webcam so there are no shadows on my face.

People will forgive poor-quality video; they won't forgive poor-quality sound. Invest in an external microphone. A good quality external microphone will be your best friend in helping you create authority in your space.

Get technical support for live workshops or webinars. Engage someone to run the back end of the show so you can focus on your presentation. Even if you are using two screens balancing the tech and the presentation is challenging. One of my first clients in my group coach program put it this way: Tech problems can be an issue for everybody and as unfair as it is, it can distract from the overall confidence level in your expertise.

There are all kinds of online tools to use when

editing your content. Most have a limited free version and are great for getting started.

FOR BEGINNERS (DRAG-AND-DROP EDITING & TEMPLATES):

Canva: https://www.canva.com/ (Free and Paid Plans): Canva offers a user-friendly interface with drag-and-drop editing and a vast library of free and paid templates specifically designed for video creation. It's perfect for beginners who want to create simple yet visually appealing videos with minimal technical knowledge.

Biteable: https://biteable.com/ (Free and Paid Plans): Biteable is another excellent option for beginners. It boasts a wide variety of eye-catching templates, stock footage, and animation tools, allowing users to create professional-looking explainer videos or social media ads.

FOR INTERMEDIATE USERS (MORE EDITING FLEXIBILITY):

WeVideo: https://www.wevideo.com/ (Free and Paid Plans): WeVideo offers a good balance between ease of use and editing flexibility. It provides a timeline interface for more control over video editing, along with pre-made templates and royalty-free media assets to enhance your creations.

Powtoon: https://www.powtoon.com/ (Free and Paid Plans): Powtoon is a great tool for creating animated presentations and explainer videos. It offers a user-friendly interface with drag-and-drop functionality and pre-built animations, making it ideal for beginners who want to add some animation flair to their videos.

FOR MOBILE EDITING APPS (BEGINNER TO INTERMEDIATE):

CapCut: (Free): CapCut is a free mobile editing app by ByteDance, the same company behind TikTok. It offers a surprisingly robust set of features for its mobile format, including easy-to-use editing tools, trendy transitions and effects, and text overlays. It's a great option for creating engaging social media videos on the go.

ClipCut: (Free): ClipCut is another free mobile editing app with a simple and intuitive interface. It allows for basic editing functions like trimming, splitting, and merging clips, as well as adding text, stickers, and music. It's a good choice for quick and easy video edits.

Opus Clips: (Free): Opus Clips is another free mobile editing app with a focus on social media video creation. It offers a wide range of editing tools, templates, and music tracks specifically designed for creating short, eye-catching videos for platforms like Instagram and TikTok.

FOR ADVANCED USERS (MORE POWERFUL EDITING TOOLS):

DaVinci Resolve: https://www.blackmagicdesign.com/event/davinciresolvedownload (Free): DaVinci Resolve is a professional-grade video editing software with a free version that offers a surprising amount of power. It has advanced editing tools, color correction features, and audio mixing capabilities, but it has a steeper learning curve compared to beginner-friendly options.

HitFilm Express: https://fxhome.com/ (Free): Similar to DaVinci Resolve, HitFilm Express offers a free version of a professional editing software. It provides powerful editing tools, motion graphics capabilities, and special effects, but requires more technical knowledge to use effectively.

ADDITIONAL OPTIONS:

Loom: https://www.loom.com/ (Free and Paid Plans): Loom is a great tool for creating quick screen recordings with webcam and microphone options. It's perfect for creating tutorials, software demos, or short explainer videos.

Mobile Editing Apps: There are also several mobile editing apps available for smartphones and tablets, such as InShot and Adobe Premiere Clip, which allow you to edit videos on the go.

CHOOSING THE RIGHT TOOL:

The best online tool depends on your specific needs, experience level, and budget. Consider the following factors when making your choice:

Ease of Use: How comfortable are you with video editing software? Spend time watching product tutorials before making a purchase. Almost everything you need to know is available in a video on YouTube. This investment of time upfront will help in the long run.

Features: What functionalities and features are important for your video project? Special effects can enhance or detract from your message. Closed captions make your videos more inclusive.

Cost: Do you need a free tool or are you willing to pay for a premium plan? My recommendation is to use it for free whenever possible.

Video Style: Are you creating simple social media videos, explainer videos, or more complex projects? An important question to ask is - what's my goal for the video? Is it to gain exposure and followers? Education my viewers on a technique? Explain a process or give a product demo.

Platform: Are you looking for a desktop application or a mobile editing app? The answer may depend on which device you will create your content. I use a combination of both my laptop and my smartphone.

By considering these factors and exploring the

options above, you can find the perfect online tool to kickstart your video creation journey.

CONCLUSION

Now that you have a lot of ideas about why a video is an important tool and how to look great on camera, take the time to create a plan of action for yourself. The following questions are designed to get you to take action and create video content for your website or social media channels.

Start by listing out the main themes of your work. My coaching program contains 3 buckets – public speaking, getting on camera, and networking.

Break down your big ideas into smaller bite-sized chunks of information to create content that is 30 to 60 seconds in length. One of my recent 30-second reminders encouraged people to smile before hitting the record button.

Use what you have to get started. I was interviewed by a podcaster not too long ago who told me when she got started, she said to herself, "I've got a Zoom account and a camera. I can create podcasts." She has grown her following from zero to thousands in a year. The important thing is to start. The only impossible journey is one you never begin. Adopt Nike's advertising mantra: Just Do It!

Take action when you feel stuck. Write 3 points on a piece of paper, open the camera app on your phone, hit record video, and talk for a minute about those three points. There is no requirement to use what you've created. You never know what you can do until you take action.

Partner with someone who has the same goal of creating video content and checking in every week. Share what you've learned, where you need help, and your plans for the following week. More often than not we break promises made to ourselves. When we tell someone else what we are going to do we are likely to make it happen.

CHAPTER 6

PUBLIC SPEAKING POWER: CRAFTING A COMPELLING MESSAGE AND DELIVERING IT WITH IMPACT

> "There is no greater agony than bearing an untold story inside you. Speak up and share your truth." - Maya Angelou

Public speaking is not just about sharing information; it's about crafting a message that resonates, captivates, and, most importantly, reflects the authentic you. In the next few pages, we're going to unravel the secrets of Public Speaking Power – a journey that will empower you to conquer your fears and share your story with unwavering confidence.

Picture this: You, center stage, delivering a message that not only educates but leaves an indelible mark on your audience. Whether you're addressing a small group or a massive audience, this chapter is designed to equip you with the tools, strategies, and mindset shifts needed to own that stage.

We'll start by understanding your audience because, let's face it, they're the heartbeat of your speech. Then, we'll dive into the art of crafting a message that not only speaks to them but speaks through you. We'll tackle the nitty-gritty of speechwriting techniques, the nuances of effective presentation, and even dive into the often-nerve-wracking Q&A sessions. The key to a successful speech is a powerful opening and a closing that leaves your audience wanting more.

And here's the secret sauce – it's not just about conquering fears; it's about thriving in the spotlight and embracing the opportunities that come with it. Get ready to craft messages that resonate, deliver them with impact, and most importantly, step into the spotlight with absolute certainty. Your voice matters, and it's time for the world to hear it loud and clear.

UNDERSTANDING YOUR AUDIENCE

Forget age, location, and income. Your audience is more than just demographics. They're real people with dreams, anxieties, and challenges you can connect with. The deeper you understand their aspirations and pain points, the better you can tailor your message to resonate. Think of it as psychographics – the "why" behind the "who." It's about values, interests, and motivations.

Odds are, you can connect with their narrative because, at some point, you were part of that group. You can easily put yourself in your audience's shoes, feeling what they feel and seeing the world through their eyes. Imagine their fears, hopes, and aspirations. By empathizing with their experiences, you gain invaluable insights into their emotional landscape. Whether they're grappling with uncertainty, seeking inspiration, or yearning for validation, your ability to empathize allows you to speak directly to their hearts. Remember, empathy is not just understanding; it's about genuinely caring and resonating with their journey. As you craft your message, infuse it with empathy, showing your audience that you're not just there to inform but to uplift and support them on their path.

I vividly remember giving a presentation in a college class. As all eyes were trained on me, I could feel the heat creeping up my chest and expanding across my face. I was bright red, revealing my anxiety. Afterwards, the well-meaning professor suggested I wear a high-collar blouse or turtleneck during presentations so that my apprehension would not show. We've all been there, navigating the intricacies of self-expression and overcoming hurdles. I learned to use the power of breathing exercises to keep myself calm and reduce my anxiety. No more turning red!

SURVEYS AND FEEDBACK

Using tools such as Survey Monkey before you step out on stage or Slido.com during your presentation will bring you a wealth of information about your audience. A well-crafted survey allows you to tap into the collective wisdom of your audience, understanding their burning questions, preferences, and expectations. Real-time feedback not only empowers your listeners by making them active participants but also provides you with valuable insights into the pulse of the room. This collaborative approach not only tailors your content to their specific needs but also reinforces a sense of shared ownership, transforming your speech into a collective experience. Embrace the power of interaction, turning your audience into partners in the journey of discovery and growth.

A word of caution if you are using an engagement tool in front of a live audience. Check and double-check your tech! Ask and answer the following questions:

1. Is there good Wi-Fi in the auditorium or meeting room?
2. Will participants have their smartphones with them?
3. Will your audience understand how to use the tool to interact with you on stage?

Failing to set up technology tools beforehand is a recipe for disaster. I observed the calamity that happened to a seasoned speaker when he failed to do this before his performance. It was all people talked about at dinner that evening. Not the impression he wanted to leave, I'm sure.

CULTURAL SENSITIVITY

Forget the "when in Rome" approach. Your audience isn't a monolith; it's a vibrant tapestry of backgrounds, values, and traditions. Cultural sensitivity is key to honoring this richness. It's more than awareness – it's actively seeking to understand cultural nuances. This allows you to tailor your message to resonate across boundaries.

To become a culturally sensitive speaker there are a few practices you can incorporate when developing your material.

Research your audience: Learn about their backgrounds and potential sensitivities. The prior section gave a couple of ideas about how to gather information about your audience. This cannot be over-emphasized. Failure to understand your audience is the number one reason speakers are not invited back by a meeting planner. This is the foundation of your presentation and will make the difference between a bland, boring presentation and one that has the potential for a standing ovation.

Mind your language: Avoid idioms or references that might be confusing or offensive. Familiarize yourself with cultural taboos to avoid inadvertently causing discomfort. This can include topics of conversation, gestures, or even humor that might be inappropriate in certain cultural contexts.

Be inclusive: Use examples and stories that reflect your audience's diversity. Whenever possible, incorporate local examples and references. This not only enhances the relevance of your message but also shows a genuine interest in and knowledge of the local culture.

Be adaptable: Some cultures may value directness, while others prefer a more indirect approach. Flexibility in your communication style demonstrates cultural awareness. Some cultures prioritize punctuality, while others may have a more flexible approach. Respect for these differences demonstrates cultural sensitivity.

Visuals: It is not only the photos or images you use on the screen, but also the picture you paint with the language you use in your presentation. Images, examples, and references should be diverse and representative of the audience. This not only fosters inclusivity but also enhances relatability.

Cultural sensitivity is a continual learning process, and your commitment to it can significantly enhance the impact of your message. But simply being aware of differences isn't enough. To truly empower others, we must strive to create an environment where everyone feels seen, heard, and respected. This means actively seeking out diverse perspectives to enrich your content and challenge your assumptions. It's about using inclusive language that resonates with a broad audience, avoiding stereotypes and generalizations.

When people from different backgrounds feel their experiences are acknowledged and valued, they become more receptive to your message. This fosters a sense of trust and connection, allowing your coaching to have a deeper and more lasting impact. Remember, cultural sensitivity is a journey, not a destination. Embrace the opportunity to learn and grow alongside your audience, and you'll find your presentations not only more effective but also more rewarding.

ADDRESS APPREHENSION

Everyone hesitates before leaping to change. It doesn't matter what your field of expertise is; your audience will have some form of apprehension as it relates to transforming their lives. That's perfectly normal!

Instead of seeing these fears as roadblocks, let's reframe them as opportunities for personal and professional growth. Facing and overcoming these fears can lead to a significant upgrade in your skills, a boost in confidence, and even open doors to entirely new possibilities.

Here's the thing: I've been there too. When I first started down the road of improving my ability to speak and grow a coaching practice around this topic, I had my own set of fears and doubts. One of the first times I attended a chapter meeting at the National Speakers Association (NSA) they were offering a program called Pro-Track. The goal was to help you build your presentation skills alongside a speaking business. The program was led by chapter members who were all Certified Speaking Professionals (CSP), a hard-earned credential in the industry. I was hesitant, it was a large investment of time and money. As I was discussing my hesitation with another potential member he said to me, "I'm battling cancer, and I'm not certain how much longer I'm going to be around. However, if I'm ready to commit, surely you can be too. You are younger and healthier. I'm certain you'll never regret making this investment in your future self." I signed up that day. And he was right, I've always been glad I stepped forward, believed in myself, and took the necessary action to move forward.

The good news? You're not alone in this. Countless others have successfully navigated through similar fears and achieved incredible results. Let's look at Sarah, a talented graphic designer who dreamed of starting her own freelance business. However, she was crippled by fear of self-promotion and imposter syndrome. What if her work wasn't good enough? What if nobody hired her? Sarah overcame these anxieties by taking a public speaking course to hone her presentation skills. She also joined online communities for freelance designers, gaining valuable advice and building a network of support. Today, Sarah runs a thriving freelance business, landing dream projects and confidently showcasing her talent to the world.

COMMON MISCONCEPTIONS

Just like any other industry, public speaking has its fair share of common myths that have persisted over time, shaping perceptions, and influencing behavior. These myths often stem from historical misconceptions and societal beliefs about communication and performance. Throughout history, public speaking has been surrounded by myths and legends, fueled by fears of judgment, rejection, and failure. From the notion that only natural-born orators can excel to the belief that nerves are a sign of weakness, these myths have stopped many from fully embracing their potential. In this section, we debunk these longstanding misconceptions and offer a fresh perspective to approach public speaking with confidence, authenticity, and resilience.

MISCONCEPTION: PUBLIC SPEAKING IS ONLY FOR EXTROVERTS

Reality: Introverts can be highly effective speakers. Public speaking is a skill that can be developed by individuals across the introversion-extroversion spectrum. Someone who has made an impact on my life is Dr. Ivan Misner, the founder of Business Network International. He refers to himself as a selective extrovert. His natural tendency is one of introversion, however, when he steps in front of an audience, he is gregarious and animated. It is not phony; he authentically engages the audience leaving them wanting more. You too can learn to embrace your inner extrovert when you step in front of a crowd.

MISCONCEPTION: GOOD SPEAKERS NEVER GET NERVOUS

Reality: Nervousness is a natural part of public speaking, even for experienced speakers. It's about managing and channeling that energy positively rather than eliminating it. Learn to reframe nerves into excitement. Think about the most engaging speakers you've seen. They channeled any anxiety they had before stepping on stage into excitement.

The renowned educator and speaker, Sir Ken Robinson, known for his TED Talk "Do Schools Kill Creativity?" and his work on education reform, admitted to experiencing stage fright earlier in his career. He shared that he overcame it by focusing on the message he wanted to convey and the importance of the ideas he was presenting.

MISCONCEPTION: MEMORIZATION EQUALS SUCCESS

Reality: While some level of preparation is essential, rigid memorization can make a speaker sound robotic. Authenticity and flexibility are key for connecting with an audience. A lot of the work I do is helping coaches practice their presentation, so they become confident and comfortable sharing their presentation. Rehearse the words out loud so you can hear the ebb and flow of your content. Make a recording on your smartphone and play it back. Practice is key to a confident and polished presentation. The more you rehearse your speech, the more comfortable you'll become with the material.

Before delivering his iconic "I Have a Dream" speech during the March on Washington for Jobs and Freedom in 1963, Martin Luther King Jr. extensively rehearsed his message. He worked on the speech's structure, wording, and delivery to ensure its powerful impact. The result was a speech that not only inspired the thousands present but also became a defining moment in the civil rights movement.

MISCONCEPTION: PUBLIC SPEAKING IS ABOUT TALKING, NOT LISTENING

Reality: Effective public speaking involves active listening to the needs and reactions of the audience. It's a two-way communication process, not just a monologue. One technique I've used is inviting the audience to turn to their neighbor and discuss the point in my presentation or answer a question on the screen. Once they've shared for a couple of minutes, I ask for a few volunteers to report on the discussion.

During a leadership development workshop, I initiated a thought-provoking dialogue centered on conquering workplace obstacles. Rather than merely lecturing, I asked participants to interact with one another, fostering a dynamic exchange of ideas and experiences. The room came alive with vibrant discussions as individuals eagerly shared their triumphs, setbacks, and insights. This collaborative atmosphere not only enriched the learning experience but also empowered each participant to collect valuable lessons from their peers' diverse perspectives.

Asking for volunteers to report back added an extra layer of engagement. One participant, initially hesitant to speak in front of the group, bravely shared a powerful anecdote about overcoming a professional hurdle. The atmosphere shifted from a traditional lecture to a collaborative exchange of ideas. The audience not only absorbed my key points but also enriched the session with their collective wisdom. This experience reinforced the transformative potential of turning a presentation into a dialogue, fostering a shared space for learning and growth.

MISCONCEPTION: SLIDES ARE THE PRESENTATION

Reality: Slides should enhance, not replace, your presentation. A well-crafted message and engaging delivery are fundamental; slides should be supportive visual aids. Simple, clear visuals enhance your message without distracting your audience. Focus on functionality over fancy animations or excessive clutter.

Beware – your audience will read any words you put on the slide. When your audience is reading the words on your slides, they are not listening to what you are saying. As humans, we cannot focus on two cognitive tasks at once. We won't hear what's being said or we will miss what we need to read. Keep your slides to under 6 words and use images that connect to your point. Use a large legible font that can be seen from the back of the room. Few things are more frustrating to an audience than complicated illegible slides.

MISCONCEPTION: YOU MUST BE PERFECT

Reality: Perfection is an unrealistic standard. Audiences connect more with authentic, imperfect speakers. If you make a mistake, shrug it off and move on. Even seasoned speakers occasionally stumble at the microphone. Embrace mistakes as opportunities for growth. Strive for improvement each time you step out on stage.

Early in my career, I found myself in front of a large audience, passionate about delivering a flawless presentation. As I made my key points, a minor slip of the tongue occurred, causing a momentary pause in the room.

Rather than dwelling on the mistake, I chose to acknowledge it with a light-hearted comment, inviting a shared chuckle from the audience. Surprisingly, that moment of imperfection became a bridge between us. The atmosphere transformed from a formal lecture to an authentic, human interaction.

After the session, attendees approached me, expressing appreciation for the genuine connection established during the talk. It was a powerful lesson: perfection might be an unattainable goal, but authenticity and the ability to navigate mistakes gracefully can create a far more meaningful and memorable experience for both speaker and audience alike. Remember, it's not about avoiding missteps but about turning them into stepping stones on your journey toward becoming an even more compelling and relatable speaker.

MISCONCEPTION: PUBLIC SPEAKING IS INHERENTLY BORING

Reality: Public speaking is an art form. Dynamic delivery, storytelling, and interactive elements can make presentations engaging and memorable. Strategic pauses can be powerful tools. They allow your key points to sink in, build anticipation, and even add emphasis. Don't be afraid of comfortable silence. People like stories. Never make a point without a story and never tell a story without a point.

One of my clients used this approach in her pitch to a large corporate client. After our coaching session, she reworked the proposal, she was preparing for a large corporate client. She integrated stories into each of the data points in her pitch deck. She told me later she believed that was the secret to her success in winning the contract.

MISCONCEPTION: YOU NEED TO PLEASE EVERYONE

Reality: It's impossible to please everyone. Focus on delivering value to your target audience and staying true to your message. Instead of a generic speech, speak directly to the needs and interests of your target audience. What are their pain points? What knowledge gaps do they have?

Let the audience know what they will gain from listening to you. Highlight key learnings or actionable steps they can take after the presentation. You might know the old adage, tell them what you are going to tell them, tell them then tell them what you've told them.

Anticipate your audience's potential objections or questions and address them head-on during your speech. Remember, the people in the room came to hear you for a reason – they're likely your ideal client or someone interested in your topic.

Don't be afraid to challenge your audience. Growth often comes from stepping outside one's comfort zone. Even if your message challenges some preconceived notions, it can still be valuable.

PRACTICE EQUALS PROGRESS

Public speaking is a skill that can be learned and improved through practice. Even the most captivating speakers started somewhere, likely nervous and inexperienced. Growth comes through experience and continuous development. Just like learning to play an instrument, even those who seem naturally gifted honed their craft through dedication. Small, consistent steps will lead to gains and improvements in the long run. Throughout history, there are many examples of people who overcame a speech impediment to be powerful communicators including:

- Demosthenes: A renowned Athenian orator in ancient Greece, Demosthenes is famous for overcoming a stammer by practicing with pebbles in his mouth.
- King George VI: King of the United Kingdom during World War II, King George VI battled a stutter that he addressed with the help of speech therapist Lionel Logue, a story depicted in the film "The King's Speech."
- Mel Tillis: This country music legend had a distinctive stutter that he incorporated into his singing style. He even wrote a song about it called "Stutterin' Boy."
- James Earl Jones: The iconic voice of Darth Vader, James Earl Jones, struggled with a

stutter throughout his youth. He eventually overcame it through dedication to acting and poetry recitation.

These individuals demonstrate the power of perseverance and dedication to become a powerful orator. Public speaking can be learned by anyone willing to put in the effort.

STORIES AND EXAMPLES

Bring your message to life by weaving in real-life stories and examples that resonate with your audience's experiences. Whether it's a personal anecdote, a case study, or a relatable scenario, these stories serve as powerful illustrations that go beyond mere information delivery. Humanizing your message through stories not only captures the audience's attention but also creates a lasting impact on their memory. Consider moments when you faced challenges, learned valuable lessons, or celebrated successes. By sharing authentically, you invite your audience into your world, fostering a connection that transcends the stage. These real-life narratives become the threads that weave your message into the fabric of their own stories, making your presentation not just informative but deeply relatable and, ultimately, unforgettable.

Be Genuine. Authenticity builds trust. Share real experiences, vulnerabilities, and lessons learned.

Authenticity resonates with people and makes your story relatable.

Keep it Concise. While it's essential to include relevant details, avoid overwhelming your audience with too much information. Keep your story focused on key points that reinforce your message.

Use your story strategically and incorporate it into branding: Integrate your signature story into your branding materials, website, and marketing collateral. Adapt your story for different contexts, such as networking events, client meetings, or presentations.

Each story can explore personal and professional growth, the power of connection, and the transformative nature of coaching and consulting relationships. Below are a list of prompts for stories within your signature story. Tell your audience about a time when:

Share the pivotal moment or experience that led you to become a coach or consultant. What was the turning point that ignited your passion for helping others?

- Client Transformation. Narrate a specific client success story. Describe the challenges they faced, the solutions you provided, and the transformative results they experienced.
- Learning from Failure. Share a personal or professional failure that taught you valuable lessons. How did this setback shape your approach to coaching or consulting?

- Unexpected Insights. Recount a moment when you discovered an unexpected insight or strategy that significantly impacted your coaching or consulting approach. How did this revelation change your perspective?
- Overcoming Doubt: Describe a time when you doubted your abilities as a coach or consultant. What steps did you take to overcome these doubts, and what did you learn from the experience?
- Innovative Solutions: Tell a story about a unique or unconventional solution you developed for a client. How did you come up with the idea, and what were the results?
- Collaborative Success: Share a story highlighting the power of collaboration. How did working with others, whether clients or colleagues, contribute to a successful outcome?
- Navigating Change: Narrate a story about guiding a client through a significant period of change. How did you help them navigate uncertainty, and what were the positive outcomes?
- Personal Growth: Discuss a moment of personal growth that directly influenced your coaching or consulting philosophy. How has your own development enhanced your ability to assist others?

- Impact Beyond Business: Share a story that illustrates the broader impact of your coaching or consulting beyond the professional realm. How have you seen positive changes ripple into other aspects of clients' lives?

MASTER THE ART & SCIENCE OF HUMOR

Mastering the art and science of using humor in a presentation can significantly enhance your ability to connect with your audience and make your message memorable. As humorist Art Buchwald once said, "I learned quickly that when I made others laugh, they liked me." Remember that not every presentation requires humor, and it's essential to gauge the appropriateness of humor based on the context and subject matter. Additionally, always be sensitive to cultural differences and avoid humor that could be offensive or exclusionary. Developing your humor skills takes practice, so don't be afraid to experiment and learn from your experiences.

In addition to reading books or viewing YouTube videos, taking an improv class is a great way to learn the elements of humor. Our local community theater offers classes, and I've always been glad I enrolled in the introductory session. While I'll never be a comedian, the class was a lot of fun and helped me develop my humor skills.

AUTHENTICITY IS KEY: AVOID APPROPRIATION

New speakers sometimes fall into the trap of borrowing stories without attribution. Imagine my mentor's shock when she heard her signature story delivered verbatim at a conference! Borrowing is fine, but only with proper credit. Aesop's Fables, Grimm's Fairy Tales, and Hans Christian Andersen offer a treasure trove of illustrative stories. Just remember to acknowledge the source and make the story your own by weaving it seamlessly into your message.

CONCLUSION

Most of my jobs in corporate America have required me to present to groups of employees on a variety of topics. One of the early presentations I learned to give was on stress management. The company I worked for required me to hand out feedback cards and ask audience members to fill them out. It wasn't until I received audience feedback that said my presentation was dry and boring, I began to learn about storytelling and why it made a difference. I honed my craft. I joined Toastmasters International and followed their process to earn my competent Toastmaster certificate Lucky for me one of the members of my chapter was a master storyteller and she took me under her wing. Much of what I've shared with you in this chapter is what I learned from personal experience. My goal is to encourage you to develop your personal story, use stories as illustrations to support data, and deliver the story in a way that is unique to you. Avoid being a copycat. Create your style that will resonate with the audience you serve. Public speaking isn't just about delivering information – it's about crafting an experience that lingers in hearts and minds, fostering growth, understanding, and shared moments of inspiration.

SUMMARY

My hope is that by now your confidence is growing because you understand the value of a growth mindset and are using affirmations on a daily basis. The feelings of confidence come after stepping up and taking action. Get comfortable being uncomfortable and you will command attention with your presentations. The story you tell yourself becomes your reality. Henry Ford said it best: If you think you can or if you think you can't either way you are right. Our mind has the power to make our life a wonderful place to live or a prison where there is no hope. My sincere hope is that you are choosing to live a life filled with positive energy. A life where you share the message you were born to share.

Facing the camera lens may bring up thoughts of imposter syndrome and pressure to be perfect. Look back at the early work of any social media influencer you follow, and you will recognize we all start somewhere. The goal is improvement, striving for excellence, not perfection. You have an important story to tell, and people are waiting to hear it. Don't deprive your audience of that opportunity.

Anyone with a smartphone can create video content for their website or social media. The technology available to simplify and amplify telling your story is readily available and ever changing. That makes creating content faster, easier, and less expensive than ever before. Try out new techniques and see what aligns with your brand. Be true to who you are when creating content and mastering the software platforms that align with your message.

Remember you have an important message to share. Your story is unlike anyone else's and only you can tell it. I use two questions to help me stay focused and engaged with the work I do – if not now, when? If not you, who? Building a business requires daily action. While it is true the journey of 1000 miles begins with a single step, the journey won't be complete unless you continue stepping forward each and every day. I'm not suggesting you never take a day off or enjoy some of the fruits of your labor. The essence of entrepreneurship is the freedom to choose when, where and how you work. What I am saying is practice and preparation are ongoing.

Think of creating and presenting your story like a play on Broadway. The playwright, director and actors all have work to do every day before the curtain comes up on opening night. The production will proceed as scheduled, with however many performances have been planned. The show closes and the sequence starts all over again with another production. Presenting your business message to a group, no matter what the size, is similar to preparing for opening night and the run of the show. It takes time, energy, and effort to arrive at the place where the curtain rises, and the show begins. The effort is maintained throughout the performance until the show closes. Each performance may change slightly, modifications made based on input from the director until the curtain falls after each performance.

It is my fervent belief you picked up a copy of this book because you have a desire to share your story with the world. The quickest, easiest, and least expensive way to do that is with a powerful presentation using a simple webcam. Since you've invested time in reading, please take the time to implement the recommendations made in the preceding chapters. Your message is worth sharing!

PART 3

CONNECTING AND ENGAGING WITH YOUR AUDIENCE

In the journey of sharing your voice and building your brand and your business we've covered a lot of ground. From mastering your mindset and creating compelling content it is time now to discover how to connect with your audience to make a difference. There are a variety of ways to engage with and build a community of loyal brand followers. Several years ago a business colleague of mine invited me to his workshop on using cold-calling tactics to grow my business. Try as I might, I just could not bring myself to consistently pick up the phone and "dial for dollars". For years I have been immersed in learning how to use word of mouth marketing to grow my business, and that is where I stayed and what I will share with you in Chapter 7 on networking.

People often misunderstand networking, thinking it is some kind of get-rich-quick scheme. Networking is not necessarily easy. You need to surround yourself with people who are willing and able to refer to your business. When it comes to growing any business, nothing is easy. Referrals will not fall from the sky even if you have a network of influential people. You need to work - your network, and that takes a plan of action and the discipline to implement the plan.

Any time you attend a networking event, do so with two goals in mind, who you can meet and how you can help them. Yes, I said how you can help them, not how they can help you. We often look at life from a what's in it for me perspective. Switch up your thinking to what can I give as opposed to what can I get. It is a counterintuitive approach for most, it certainly was for me early in building my networking skills. However it has served me well.

Since early 2020 when COVID 19 reared its ugly head much of what we do to grow our customer base is online. According to The Marketing Helpline, in 2020, an estimated 3.6 billion people were using social media worldwide when just 10 years earlier social media was much less crowded and complicated. It was a place to stay in touch with loved ones, it lacked sponsored posts and influencer marketing was not yet born. Over the years social media grew to a media outlet where you can brand your business and even conduct transactions. And not interacting with your audience on social platforms creates a serious case of FOMO (fear of missing out) to most coaches.

The Wealth Preservation Podcast featured Savion Nehemiah of 413 Media, who likened entrepreneurship to being a gambler. The entrepreneur places bets every day on where they are going to spend their time, energy, and effort to grow their business. Some bets will pay off, some won't, yet we continue to place bets. The savvy entrepreneur has a process to evaluate and analyze those bets and uses the information to move their business forward. They don't retreat and give up; they adjust and move forward. They find others who've led the way and model their tactics and strategies.

They also know the unexpected is bound to happen and being resilient is a key factor in success. Take for example the resiliency of Thomas Edison. When his life's work exploded in 1914 and fire raged through the plant, he advised his son to get his mother and gather her friends because "They'll never see a fire like this again!" Can you imagine, at the age of 67, watching your entire life's work go up in smoke? Edison took it all in stride and with the fire barely cold, he told his employees he would rebuild and explained, "You can always make capital out of disaster. We've just cleared out a bunch of old rubbish! We'll build bigger and better on these ruins."

Most people would be devastated watching their life's work go up in flames. Yet Edison was willing to begin again and build his business back from the ashes, so to speak. In January 2022, entrepreneur Reid Hoffman tweeted "I believe starting a company is like jumping off a cliff and assembling a plane on the way down -- your willingness to jump is your most valuable asset as an entrepreneur." I doubt there is a more terrifying spot to be in. Not knowing if you will succeed in creating a craft that will propel you upward or if you will crash and burst into flames. According to data from the Bureau of Labor Statistics, as reported by Fundera, approximately 20 percent of small businesses fail within the first year. By the end of the second year, 30 percent of businesses will have failed. By the end of the fifth year, about half will have failed. And by the end of the decade, only 30 percent of businesses will remain — a 70 percent failure rate.[1]

Yet knowing all these statistics, I started my coaching practice, and you may have too, since you are reading this book. Yes! There is a lot of data to suggest things won't work out in our favor, however, there are just as many stories of people who have overcome tremendous odds and created a business to fund the life they love. A famous example is Sir Richard Branson, who struggled with dyslexia during his childhood, which affected his academic performance. Throughout his early career, Branson has demonstrated a knack for taking calculated risks and challenging the status quo. Branson's early life experiences, marked by his struggles with dyslexia and his entrepreneurial endeavors, instilled in him a sense of resilience, creativity, and a willingness to push boundaries. These qualities would later define his approach to business and contribute to his success as a serial entrepreneur and philanthropist.

You may have a desire to grow an empire as large as Sir Richard's or simply build a business to support you and your family comfortably. My goal is to provide a resource for you on your journey to build your speaking skills to build your business whatever the size and shape of your heart's desire.

CHAPTER 7

NETWORKING FOR IMPACT: LEVERAGING STORYTELLING TO BUILD RELATIONSHIPS AND ATTRACT CLIENTS

> "Your network is your net worth." - Porter Gale

Marketing is the heartbeat of any thriving business—it's the pulse that attracts attention, generates interest, and ultimately compels action. It's the art of making your presence known, your value understood, and your solutions sought after. But it's more than just ads and promotions; it's about forging connections, nurturing relationships, and positioning yourself as the answer to your clients' needs.

There is more "noise" in the marketplace than ever before. Competition is fierce and attention spans are fleeting. Mastering the art of marketing is essential for anyone seeking to make a meaningful impact. It's about more than just selling a service or product; it's about creating a compelling story that resonates with your audience on a deep, emotional level.

You have several choices when it comes to marketing and selling your services; cold calls, paid advertising, or word of mouth sometimes called referral marketing. A YouTube search will reveal several experts who recommend cold calling and demonstrate the techniques required to be effective and book sales calls. Ads on Google or Facebook are costly; roughly $3000 a month over a series of months for the ad to produce results. Referral marketing is about building relationships with other professionals who are willing and able to refer to you and your business. In my opinion, it is one of the least expensive forms of marketing. It does require time and attention to create a network that works for you. This chapter is designed to be your guide in building your network alongside building your business.

Three people share similar philosophies when it comes to building your business by referral. First is Zig Ziglar, speaker, author, and consummate sales professional who said - "You can have everything in life you want if you will just *help* enough *other people* get what they want." Dr. Ivan Misner the founder of Business Network International (BNI) believes in the concept of Givers Gain, and finally, Bob Berg wrote a wonderful book entitled *The Go-Giver* a story about a salesman, Joe, desperate for success and learns the value of the proverb "give and you shall receive". Please keep the idea of giving before receiving as you read and implement the ideas in this chapter. We will cover 3 main points: building, working, and maintaining your network.

BUILD IT THEY WILL COME

In the movie The Field of Dreams the main character plows under his farmland and builds a baseball field in hopes that people will visit. He is met with criticism from almost everyone until (spoiler alert) at the very end of the movie you see a line of cars driving towards the farm leaving the impression he succeeded after all.

Building your network is similar in a way because you will put in a lot of effort upfront, and it takes a while to see results. During my time as a director for BNI, I observed many sales professionals and business owners who would join a chapter and expect it to rain referrals. That is not how doing business by referral works. Referral marketing is not a get-rich-quick scheme. It takes time, energy, and effort to build a profitable network. That being said, let's get started building your network.

WHO DO YOU KNOW?

We all have a circle of influence, family, friends, neighbors, and co-workers. People we interact with for a variety of reasons. Maybe you are thinking, "I don't know anyone who can help me build my coaching practice" While that might be a true statement it is the people they know that you want to tap into. Research suggests that all of us know about 250 people, so start with who you already know and build from there.

Open a spreadsheet on your computer and create the following column headings: Name, Business Name or Profession, Relationship, Email, Phone, Contact Date, Notes, Follow-up date, Next Action.

- **Name** – you may want to break this into First Name in one column and Last Name in another so you can sort the data alphabetically.
- **Business Name or Profession** – this could be 2 columns as well, for example, my business name is Leslie Fiorenzo Enterprises, LLC. That does not tell you much about what I do unless you enter "Business Presentation Coach" in the Profession column next to the Business Name column.
- **Relationship** – make a note of how you know this person, be it your brother-in-law (yes you can list family even if you don't have a family business) a former work colleague, or a customer – you get the idea.
- **Email & Phone** – pretty self-explanatory, however, if you know both their business and personal contact details add them both so all your data is in one place.

- **Contact date** – this is the date you first emailed or called.
- **Notes** – what happened as the result of your outreach. Fill in as much detail as needed to help you remember the conversation and the next steps on your part.
- Follow-up **date** – this is the date you set as a task or reminder in your calendar system.
- **Next action** – what is the next step that you need to take in building the relationship.

CIRCLE OF INFLUENCE: WHO I KNOW

NAME	RELATIONSHIP	CONTACT INFO	DATE OF CONTACT	NOTES
ADAM GRANT				
JOHN SMITH				
SALLY DOW				
LINDA JONES				
MARY TRAINER				
JACK ANDERSON				

Now that your spreadsheet is complete, add time in your calendar to work your network. Make and keep an appointment with yourself to do the outreach to the people on the list. Treat this appointment like you would time scheduled for a valued client. Avoid breaking the appointment. Most people have great intentions when it comes to taking action and implementing the information they've consumed. It has been my experience that unless it is on my calendar it probably won't happen.

And speaking of calendars, enroll in a system that makes scheduling time with you easy. There are any number of free versions available. This way when you are connecting with people you can send them a link to your calendar, and they can schedule a time that fits their schedule. It eliminates all the back and forth of emails and phone calls to set up a meeting.

NETWORKING GROUPS

Dr. Ivan Misner, a pioneer in the field of networking, founded BNI (Business Network International), the world's largest business networking organization. Ecademy refers to him as the "Father of Modern Networking. With over three decades of experience, Dr. Misner has been instrumental in revolutionizing the way professionals connect and collaborate globally. His insights into the power of networking, combined with his passion for helping others succeed, have made him a sought-after authority in the realm of business relationships and networking strategies. According to Dr. Ivan Misner, we should consider joining three types of groups: community service such as Rotary International, soft contact groups like your local chamber of commerce and hard contact groups like BNI where only one person in the profession is allowed to join. A simple way to meet new people to add to your network is to join a group and become an active member.

Up until March of 2020, the vast majority of networking groups met in person, now the vast majority meet on a virtual platform. A Google search for virtual networking groups brought me about 220,000,000 results in 0.41 seconds. Alternately a search for networking groups near me resulted in about 245,000,000 results in 0.48 seconds. My point? There are a lot of groups to explore. Dedicate 10 minutes a day over the next week to research the groups that are a good fit for your business. Join the group, interact with the members, and attend one or two of their events, to discover if you can make a valuable contribution. The question in the back of your mind needs to be: "Can I be helpful to this group of people?" If the answer to that question is yes, then the people in the group will be able to help you. Yes, this is a counterintuitive approach. Most people think about "How can the people in the group benefit me?" Remember Zig Ziglar's sound advice at the start of the chapter. Your goal is to help people get what they want.

Even though I said joining and attending networking groups is a simple way to grow your network, for you introverts reading this book it is not the easiest way. It is not easy because it requires you to step out of your comfort zone and be visible. Introverts make great networkers because they are typically more thoughtful in their approach to situations. Extroverts tend to just show up and make things happen. An extrovert by nature, I've learned the value of planning my approach before I show up at an event to maximize the effectiveness of attending. Avoid letting your introversion be an excuse.

NETWORKING EVENTS

Networking events are happening every day, online and in person. Enough online events are happening you could turn up at one each day. Showing up at events requires time in your schedule. Be selective and focused on how you spend time. Attend events that are right for you and your business.

Some groups hold their own events. Your local chamber of commerce may conduct a monthly business mixer inviting members and non-members to show up and mingle with other businesspeople. BNI is a members only group, people may visit their weekly meetings twice before they are asked to decide about membership. Facebook has a variety of groups to join based on a variety of interests. In some cases, these groups hold networking events. One Facebook group I'm a member of has a monthly in-person networking event designed to help members enjoy social interaction and develop deeper relationships.

Attending in-person networking events can be more fun with a partner. Ask your best business buddy to attend with you and work the room together. It can be a natural way to introduce each other. After a few minutes of conversation with another attendee, you can say, "Let me introduce you to Jackie Smith, with ABC Company. She is great at what she does and knows a lot of people in the community. She's just across the room." So you walk the person over and introduce them to Jackie.

You will rarely find a buyer for your product or service at a networking event. Approach the event as an opportunity to meet new people to potentially add to your network. Set a goal to meet three new people at each event you attend. Collect their contact information so you can follow up the next day and schedule a time to explore if this person is someone you can help. Outreach to these new connections can be via email, although I prefer the old-fashioned phone call method. Either way, the message you want to convey is this: you'd like to meet to learn more about their business and how you might be able to help them. Would you have any interest in that? In your email, you can place a link to your calendar and invite them to schedule a time that is convenient for them. Your goal in this discussion is to see if there is a fit and if you can genuinely help them.

When you meet someone and get their contact information please avoid adding them to your email marketing list without their permission. Remember people are not attending the event to be sold goods or services during or after the event. As a result of getting to know you at subsequent meetings, they may visit your website and voluntarily add themselves by downloading your freebie. Let them make that decision, not you.

YOUR ELEVATOR PITCH

Networking requires you to have a short introduction to describe the product or service offered by your business. It is called an elevator pitch because it generally takes about 30 seconds to ride up or down between floors with other people. In all my years of riding elevators I don't believe I've ever seen someone use their pitch; I know I've never used mine. Nonetheless, take the time to create a 30 to 60-second infomercial about you and your business. You can pull ideas from your signature story created in Chapter 3.

Choose one of the following methods. You can change them up and see which one you like better. Experiment, have fun and stay within the time frame of 30 to 60 seconds. I've seen far too many people drone on and on when they introduce themselves. Because you never get a second chance to leave a first impression, follow the KISS principle – keep it sweet and simple!

METHOD #1 TRADITIONAL INTRODUCTION

Hello, my name is (insert your name) and (your ideal client/niche) hire me when (describe their problem). By working with me they will (describe the outcome you help them achieve). A good connection for me is (specific ask).

My example is as follows - Hi, I'm Leslie Fiorenzo and coaches hire me when they struggle with self-promotion because they fear public speaking, getting on camera or talking about their business at a networking event. I help them build their ability to speak confidently about their business in any setting. A good connection for me is Jane Doe with ABC Health Coaching.

METHOD #2 CREATE CURIOSITY

Another way to do this is to start by asking a question that describes a problem you solve in your business and then you tell them how you solve it. When you ask a question people automatically start thinking of an answer. This type of introduction engages people from the start.

You know how (insert the problem) What I do is (your solution)

I've used this model by saying – You know how most coaches struggle with self-promotion? What I do is help them improve their speaking skills so they can promote their business with absolute certainty.

METHOD #3 FULFILL A DESIRE

A third way you could introduce yourself is I help blank get blank. The first blank is your ideal customer, and the second blank is what they desire. I help coaches move from petrified to powerful when sharing their business message.

All of these examples are less than 30 seconds. The idea is to create interest, so people want to have a conversation with you at a later date. You cannot possibly close a deal using your pitch. It is simply designed to pique the listeners' curiosity and see if it makes sense to schedule a follow-up meeting.

Now that you've piqued someone's interest with your introduction, exchanged contact information, and agreed on a date to meet and learn more, you might be wondering, what are we going to talk about at this meeting? You might be thinking, "I certainly don't need to meet up and have coffee. I've got a business to run!" Of course, that's why you want an agenda anytime you meet with a networking partner. Come prepared and help them prepare as well so the time you spend together creates value for both parties.

FIRST MEETING AGENDA

This meeting is designed to do two things: get to know the other person and see if they are willing to introduce you to others and vice versa. Please avoid selling your product or service to this new business acquaintance, unless they tell you they are interested in seeing how it might work for them. I've frequently encountered people who show up to a meeting like this, immediately launching into a presentation on their product or service without any questions to discover if I even have a need or interest. Please, avoid making this mistake. The goal of any introductory meeting is to learn more about the other person if you are willing and able to refer business their way and vice-versa.

Consider the following outline or framework for your meeting:

Build rapport. Discover a bit about them. Prepare three questions to ask along with your answers to the same questions. You want the conversation to flow easily. Some sample questions to consider:

- How long have you lived in this area?
- What do you like best about your business?
- What do you like best about doing business in this area?
- What is your ideal customer?
- What can I listen for or look for to know if someone is an ideal customer for you?

Once you've established a connection you can deepen the conversation to learn more. The GAINS profile developed by BNI is a useful tool for this first meeting. G is for goals, A is for accomplishments, I is for interests, N is for networks and S is for skills. Create the outline for yourself first with your answers and send it to your networking partner in advance of the meeting. Adapt the following language into an email.

Dear (the name of your networking partner)
I am looking forward to our meeting (date & location), getting to learn more about you and your business. In order to make the best use of our time together I have attached a document we can use as an outline. I've populated my answers and attached a blank one for you to put in your information.
It would be great if you fill it out and send it back before the meeting. If not, I understand, please bring it with you when we meet.
Looking forward to seeing you soon.
Your name

Using an agenda like this will keep your meeting focused and let the other person know you are serious about building a beneficial business relationship. I am certain you have a number of friends who you can meet for coffee. This is a meeting to build a business relationship. If it turns out a friendship develops all the better.

During the time I was involved in BNI as a director, responsible for supporting 12 chapters, members would occasionally complain their 1-2-1 meetings were not producing any results, in other words, no referrals. When I'd ask them if they were using the GAINS worksheet, sharing it before the meeting, and using it as a tool for follow-up, they'd sheepishly admit they were not. Once they followed the recommendation of a focused agenda for their meeting, they began to give and receive referrals. Most meetings without an agenda are a disaster. There is no focus and no result. Your time as a business owner is too valuable to waste. Take the time before the meeting to make a plan for the discussion, share that with your networking partner, get agreement on who will do what next, and follow up, follow up, follow up!

EDUCATE YOUR NETWORK

Avoid succumbing to the myth that if you attend enough networking events people will bring you referrals. That may help build your visibility in the business community, it does not guarantee people will refer business to you. Your referral sources need to know, in detail, what to do to get a referral for you. The most effective networkers I know have created a document to share with their referral partners. Of course, it includes the name, address, email, phone number, and website for your business. It also includes instructions on what the referral partner needs to listen for or look for in order to spot a good referral for you. What is the best way for them to give you the name and contact information of the referral so you can follow up? When is the referral expecting your contact, do they have an immediate need for your service or are they simply kicking tires? Make it easy for the person to refer business to you.

THE DEPTH & BREADTH OF YOUR NETWORK

Is your network a mile wide and an inch deep? In other words, you know lots of people but not very well. Or an inch wide and a mile deep? In this case, you have fewer connections, and you know them very well. These are the people you can call on at a moment's notice and they will respond. Spend some time examining the contacts in your database. If your network is wide and shallow, what action can you take to deepen your relationships? If your network is deeply connected, are there any gaps that you need to fill? Identify the professions that could naturally refer business to you and you to them. Are they in your network or do you need to build a relationship? This will allow you to build a team of powerful alliances to refer business back and forth.

The easiest example to use is that of a mortgage broker, residential real estate broker, and an insurance agent for home & auto. These three professions can naturally refer business to one another. Additional members might include a title agent, an interior designer, a home appraiser, a handyman, lawn service to name a few. You can create powerful business allies with a group like this. Some networking experts refer to this as a power team or circle of influence. Once you create the group avoid leaving referrals to chance. Set up specific times to meet on a regular frequency to get to know the other members, share updates about your business, and exchange referrals.

Be particular about who you include in your circle. If someone cannot commit to attending the meetings regularly and contributing in a meaningful way, they are not right for your group. There are all times when we have plans and life interferes; family emergencies and client catastrophes happen upon occasion. When absences become a pattern, it is time to have a hard conversation with that individual and invite them to find a different group to attend. When you refer someone to your best customer it is a reflection of you and your business. Some people fail to realize that their actions inside the group are an indication of how they serve their clients.

Several years ago I coached a group leader who was struggling to build a network of strong connections to do business by referral. Her professional slot was filled in all the groups in town, so she wanted to build her own. In the course of our conversation, I discovered she had not taken the time to identify which professions supported her business and would be good referral sources. She was simply showing up at networking events around town with no plan and no purpose. Take the time now to create a written description of your ideal group complete with mission and goals BEFORE you begin to recruit members.

NETWORKING WORKS... IF YOU WORK IT

There are any number of ways to find people who can potentially become your customers: cold calls, advertising, or networking to find customers. Each one has merit. My personal favorite is networking because I've found it to be more comfortable and more profitable than either of the other ways. You don't have to take my word for it, try it out for yourself. There are hundreds if not thousands of events that take place in person and online each week. Do your research, find groups that resonate with you and show up to check them out. Of course, it goes without saying you will show up prepared with your 30 to 60-second elevator pitch, a goal for the number of connections you want to make, and your plan for follow-up conversations.

Decide how much time in your week you'll devote to networking. In our virtual world you could attend one event a day. All it takes is the discovery of one group to make it worth your while. Please don't expect immediate results. Rome wasn't built in a day and your network will not be either. Take daily, consistent action to connect with like-minded people. Give referrals to these people, follow up on the referrals you've given and of course the ones you receive. Expand your network with professions you don't already know to build business relationships.

Remember it isn't what you know it is who you know and not only that it is how well you know them.

CHAPTER 8

CONTENT CREATION TO ENGAGE AND BUILD A COMMUNITY

> "Content is king, but engagement is queen, and she rules the house." - Mari Smith

In this age of digital distraction, where attention spans are short and competition is fierce, creating compelling content is key to not only attracting but also retaining an audience. Your ability to connect with your audience through content is what sets you apart and builds a loyal community around your brand.

Think of the iconic brands you know like Apple, Starbucks, and most recently Taylor Swift and her loyal followers known as "Swifties". These brands have created a community, a place where people can come together to find connection, support, and shared experiences. Your goal is to create a similar following to the greatest degree possible.

Are you like me? I do have an Apple phone;

however, I don't drink Starbucks Coffee or own any of Taylor's music. However, we can learn from their strategies and tactics. Starbucks has built a loyal customer base that keeps coming back by focusing on three simple ideas: relationship building, persistence, and value creation.

Apple has masterfully built a loyal customer base using its minimalist and elegant design philosophy. Every Apple product is meticulously crafted to be user-friendly, intuitive, and reliable. Couple that with optimizing devices for smooth performance and its excellent customer service, Apple has built a cult-like following where customers stand in line for hours, if not days before a new product release to make a purchase.

And Taylor? First, she is a master storyteller, writing lyrics that resonate with fans of all ages. Then she can connect deeply with her audience during her heartfelt performances. An additional trait that makes her stand out is the hidden messages she put in her music, referred to as Easter Eggs, fans relish the opportunity to solve these puzzles, creating a sense of accomplishment and anticipation for new releases.

We can employ similar strategies to build a brand and support our following in a way that is genuine, unique, and resonates with the people we serve. Let's dive in.

UNDERSTANDING YOUR AUDIENCE

Before you can create content that resonates, you need to understand who you are speaking to. It is more than identifying the demographics of your target audience, it is about understanding their needs, interests, and pain points, and creating a buyer persona to inform your content strategy. You may recall in Chapter 2 I said, "Tailor your story to resonate with the needs and interests of your ideal client." Take the time to create a worksheet that describes both the demographics and psychographics of your ideal client. This will allow you to create a picture in your mind of the person you are talking to in your presentation. My ideal client persona's name is Sally. She is 45 years old, has been coaching for about 12 months and she feels like she is not getting any traction in her business. She is timid when it comes to sharing her message because she does not like seeing herself on camera. She has created a couple of videos. However, the videos did not get the response she expected so she stopped creating and posting video content. She is not taking consistent action to amplify her voice on social media, and she does not have any video of herself sharing her message on her website. She is about ready to give up on her business and find a job. A clear picture of the person you are creating a message for helps you connect with the audience that will resonate with your message.

This idea is counterintuitive to many because it feels

limiting. Trust me, you cannot serve everyone. Plus, you need to give your brain a specific focus. Have you ever purchased an automobile, let's say a white Honda CRV, driven it off the lot, and noticed how many other people are driving white CRVs? Once you've created your client persona you'll be able to see them everywhere in everyday life.

IDENTIFYING YOUR UNIQUE VOICE AND MESSAGE

What sets you apart from other people who do work similar to yours? Every one of us has unique gifts and talents. Each of us brings a distinct perspective to the work we do. You are not the best fit for EVERYONE, you are the best fit for your ideal client. When I first started down the entrepreneurial road this question haunted me. It wasn't until, working with my coach, I discovered answers: my 30-plus years in corporate America, training on a wide range of topics, presenting to hundreds of people in person and online, honing my craft by constantly learning and growing, surrounding myself with people who support me and challenge me to level up my game, trying new methods and ideas to see what works. I bring all of this knowledge and experience to every coaching session with every client. I was honored by one client's review when she said, "Coming into the program I felt like I was a pretty good public speaker. Since attending the sessions and doing the work, I now have some strategies that I can use to fine tune my presentations and make them better." That captures the essence of my work with clients – improvement. Small gains build over time. My best clients are the ones who are willing to take steps every day to build their speaking skills. People who take the long view know that when they put in the work today, tomorrow, and the next day, consistently taking action in a few weeks, they'll see progress.

Now it is your turn, what makes you different than others who do similar work with similar clients? Notice I did not refer to these coaches or consultants as your competitors. Why? Because I believe there is room for all of us at the table. You would not have been given your business idea if you were not meant to prosper with the idea. Set aside a few blocks of time to do this work if you have not done it before.

What knowledge, skills, and abilities can I share with my clients/customers? Many people suggest you draw 3 intersecting circles and where the circles overlap is your zone of genius.

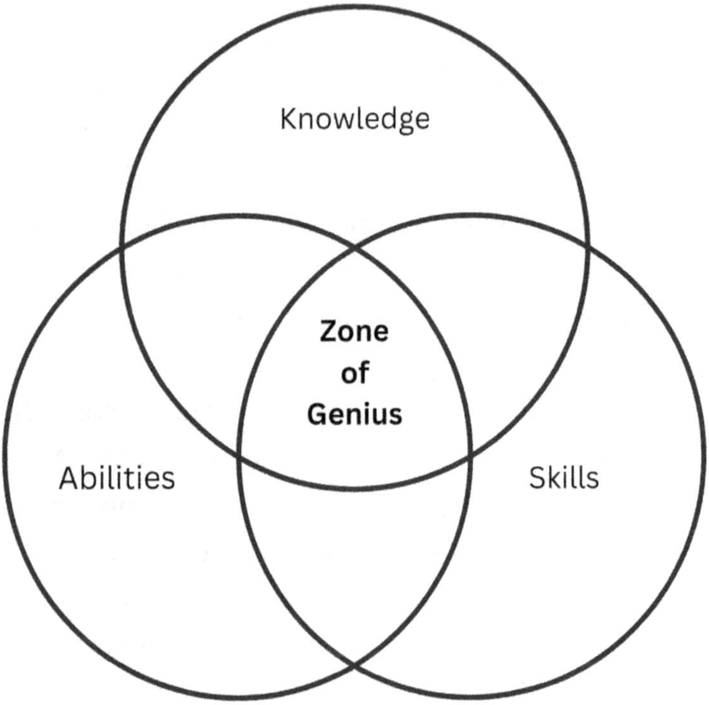

- What experience do you have?
- What is my educational background?
- What is the process or system you have used or created that will help others overcome similar challenges?
- What are your core values and how do they show up in your work?
- What is your source of inspiration? Or who is your role model?
- What feedback have you received from past clients or colleagues?

- What do you enjoy most about your work?

Be sure to save your work so you can return to it each year. Take time, annually, to review it and build on it. It can be a source of inspiration. It will help you identify areas of growth and progress. Journalling is a powerful tool to help record progress and clarify thoughts. Examples of well-known people who have kept journals include Leonardo da Vinci, Mark Twain, Steve Jobs, and Oprah Winfrey.

Your brand message needs to resonate with your following. We are not right for everyone, nor can we serve everyone. This idea is challenging for many new coaches. Remember; to infuse your personality and values into your content to attract like-minded individuals and build a strong personal brand.

CHOOSING THE RIGHT CONTENT CHANNELS

Never before have there been so many places to post and share content. Countless platforms scream for our attention in the digital landscape, so the selection of the right channels to distribute your content can seem overwhelming. However, by understanding your audience demographics, preferences, and behavior, you can strategically choose the channels that best align with your content goals and maximize your impact. Here is where research and experimentation come in. Where does your ideal client spend their digital time? LinkedIn will provide analytics and so will Google. Use these tools to help you know what posts are resonating with your audience.

Each social site has strengths and features to be leveraged to showcase your expertise and connect with your audience. Do you need a more visual platform like Instagram or Pinterest? This is where the audience persona you created will help. Select one and get started. Post content consistently, build a following, engage with them, and move on to another platform. Trying to be in too many places at once can be overwhelming and has caused many people to give up using social media entirely. No matter what some headlines or online gurus proclaim, no one built a following overnight. Small consistent action will pay off over time.

CREATING VALUABLE AND ENGAGING CONTENT

Quality is king when it comes to content creation. Sharing your expertise allows you to shine. I observed an interesting debate about the idea of giving away your best material for free. One person proclaimed that "free does not pay the bills". While that is true, how are people in the digital world going to get to know you, like you, and trust you unless you share your best material? Plus, it always surprises me when people aren't aware of something. A few weeks ago I was a workshop participant, and the speaker was explaining the boxed breathing technique. The woman next to me said, "Gosh I didn't know this." Yet boxed breathing is a technique I've used and taught for years.

A content calendar is a tool to guide content creation and track what you are sharing. When you are starting the thought of filling in all the boxes can seem daunting. Start with a calendar complete with prompts like your mission, your vision, quizzes, polls, and behind-the-scenes, tips or tricks. It is your best material broken down into small chunks. You will find one on this book's website.

Since the release of Chat GPT and other forms of AI in late 2022 there has been a debate about the using such tools. I would suppose it may be similar to when the automobile first arrived on the scene. Some saw it as a modern marvel, others that the forbearing of impending doom. I've found a product using AI that captures my voice to help me create social media content with ease. There's a link in the resource section if you are interested. My point is AI is a tool and like any other tool it takes time to master. And can be used for good or not so good. It is all in the hands of the person who wields the tool.

Use the story you created in Chapter 2 as a basis for content creation. Powerful stories build powerful brands. Your goal is to create a connection with your audience. Creating a long-lasting bond with your followers. One that is built on trust and authenticity. Be true to yourself and your values. The more scammers that show up in the digital space, the more and more skeptical people become. Couple that with the increasing volume of content and every changing algorithm you might wonder, why bother? Because, dear reader, your voice is important. And there are people out there waiting to hear from you. It is only with diligence that you will find them.

Your goal is to get your audience's attention and keep them coming back for more. Deliver content that not only connects with their needs and desires but also sparks curiosity, inspires action, and fosters a sense of belonging. When you can create compelling images in your clients' minds, share valuable insights, and engage in meaningful interactions, you can create a dynamic and immersive experience that leaves a lasting impression on your audience, driving continued engagement and loyalty to your brand.

MEASURING SUCCESS

Unless you start with a specific goal in mind for your content creation it can be hard to measure success. Each goal has a specific set of metrics often referred to as key performance indicators (KPIs). These may include metrics such as website traffic, social media engagement, email open rates, conversion rates, and customer retention rates.

By monitoring these metrics regularly using

analytics tools such as Google Analytics, social media analytics platforms, and email marketing software, you can gain valuable insights into the impact of your content on audience engagement, conversion rates, and overall business performance.

In addition to quantitative metrics, it's essential to gather qualitative feedback from your audience to understand their preferences, needs, and pain points. By actively listening to your audience and asking for their feedback, you can gain valuable insights into what resonates with them, what areas need improvement, and how you can better serve their needs through your content.

Use the data and insights from your metrics and audience feedback to refine your content strategy. This may include making adjustments to your content topics, formats, distribution channels, and messaging to better align with audience preferences and business objectives.

Think of everything as an experiment. Become a scientist, testing your hypothesis, and adjusting along the way. Experimentation is key to continuous improvement. Test different content formats, headlines, visuals, and calls to action to see what resonates best with your audience. Be open to trying new approaches and learning from both successes and failures.

Agility and adaptability are crucial qualities for success in your approach to content creation, responding quickly to changes in audience behavior, industry trends, and algorithm updates on various platforms. When you constantly monitor your metrics and audience feedback, you can be prepared to pivot your strategy as needed to stay ahead of the curve and remain relevant in the eyes of your audience.

By implementing a systematic approach to measuring success and adjusting your content strategy based on feedback and insights, you can continuously refine your approach to content creation, better serve your audience's needs, and achieve your business goals in the ever-evolving digital landscape.

CONCLUSION

Consider the stories of Gary Vee, Jenna Kutcher, and Pat Flynn as role models for perseverance in the world of content creation and social media success.

You may be familiar with Gary Vaynerchuk, also known as Gary Vee, is a serial entrepreneur, author, and speaker who rose to prominence through his content creation efforts. Born in

Babruysk, Belarus (formerly part of the Soviet Union), Gary and his family immigrated to the United States in 1978 and settled in Edison, New Jersey. Upon joining his family's wine business, Gary initially gained recognition with his video blog, Wine Library TV, where he shared wine reviews and business advice entertainingly and candidly. He later expanded his digital presence with the launch of VaynerMedia, a full-service digital agency that helps brands leverage social media and content marketing to drive business results. Gary's relentless focus on providing value to his audience through his content has not only built a massive following but has also established him as a leading authority in marketing and entrepreneurship. He is highly active on platforms like Instagram, Twitter, LinkedIn, and YouTube. He also has his website where he shares content and updates about his various ventures.

Jenna Kutcher is a photographer turned entrepreneur who has built a multi-million-dollar brand through her blog, podcast, and social media platforms. The Goal Digger Podcast, started in 2016 and hosted by Jenna, has become a top-rated show on iTunes, further solidifying her influence and impact in the online space. Growing up in Wisconsin she attended the University of Wisconsin-Stout, where she studied business marketing and entrepreneurship. Jenna's journey began when she started sharing her experiences as a wedding photographer on her blog and Instagram. Over time, she expanded her content to include topics such as entrepreneurship, personal development, and body positivity. Through her relatable and inspiring storytelling, Jenna has cultivated a loyal following of women who resonate with her message of chasing their dreams and building a life they love. Along with her podcast, you can find Jenna on Instagram, Facebook, and Twitter.

Pat Flynn is an entrepreneur and the founder of Smart Passive Income, a highly successful blog and podcast where he shares his experiences and strategies for building passive income streams online. Pat initially started his blog in 2008 to document his experiences and experiments with generating passive income online. He shared his successes and failures openly, providing valuable insights and resources for others interested in building online businesses. Through his transparent and authentic storytelling, along with valuable content and resources, he quickly gained a loyal following of entrepreneurs and aspiring online business owners. Today, Smart Passive Income has grown into a thriving online community with millions of followers, and Pat has become a trusted authority in the online business space. Pat Flynn is active on platforms like Twitter, Instagram, and LinkedIn.

I used these examples because people often view others who've made it to the proverbial top as an "overnight success". What is important to note is that in reality, each of these individuals experienced a journey filled with hard work, persistence, and strategic effort before achieving significant recognition and success. Here's a brief overview of the timelines for each:

Pat Flynn's journey to success with Smart Passive Income was anything but overnight. After being laid off from his job in 2008, he started his blog and began experimenting with various online business strategies. It took several months of consistent effort and content creation before he started to see significant traction. His podcast, which launched in 2010, also took time to gain momentum and reach a wide audience. Overall, Pat's journey to becoming a well-known figure in the online business space spanned several years of dedicated work and continuous learning.

Jenna Kutcher's rise to prominence as a podcaster and influencer was also a gradual process. She started her photography business and began sharing her journey on social media platforms like Instagram. Over time, her audience grew as she continued to provide valuable content and insights into entrepreneurship and personal development. The launch of The Goal Digger Podcast in 2016 further expanded her reach and solidified her position as a thought leader in the industry. Like Pat Flynn, Jenna's success was the result of consistent effort and a commitment to providing value to her audience over an extended period.

Gary Vaynerchuk's journey to success began with his family's wine business, Wine Library, where he gained recognition through his video blog, Wine Library TV. While he experienced some early success with his online content, it wasn't until he launched VaynerMedia in 2009 that his influence and impact truly skyrocketed. Building a successful digital agency and expanding his brand through speaking engagements, books, and social media took years of hard work, dedication, and strategic planning. Gary's "overnight success" was the culmination of decades of entrepreneurial experience and a relentless pursuit of excellence.

We can learn from and model their journeys to

success; characterized by perseverance, resilience, and a long-term commitment to their craft. Each of them invested years of effort into building their businesses and personal brands, gradually gaining traction and recognition before achieving widespread success.

SUMMARY

Author and mindset coach Devon Brough reminds us that life is hard, and we get to choose our hard. He is known for putting it this way: Marriage is hard. Divorce is hard. Choose your hard. Obesity is hard. Being fit is hard. Choose your hard. Being in debt is hard. Being financially disciplined is hard. Choose your hard. Communication is hard. Not communicating is hard. Choose your hard. Life will never be easy. It will always be hard. But we can choose our hard. Pick wisely.

I would add to his idea that whatever path in life we choose – it will be hard. Building a business is hard and so is being an employee, you get to choose your hard. Growing a business requires us to step out of our comfort zone, into a new space we've never experienced before. It is in the space outside of the familiar where we can learn to excel.

As I write this chapter March Madness is just beginning. For those of you who don't follow NCAA basketball in the US, it's a single-elimination tournament where 64 teams compete to be crowned the national champion. It's a frenzy of college basketball excitement where upsets are common, with lower-seeded teams sometimes defeating the higher-ranking favorites, which adds to the drama. What, you might be wondering, does this have to do with the subject at hand? Let me explain. These 64 teams represent the best of the best college basketball has to offer. Players and their coaches put in long hours of practice and preparation both on and off the court. In some games, it comes down to the final seconds with a game-winning shot advancing that team to the next level of play. What people don't see are the hours the athlete spends in the gym practicing free throws or in the weight room building muscle in the wind sprints to increase endurance. It is similar to the hours you spend meeting with potential networking partners, evaluating fit, and building the relationship. The research that goes into creating your ideal client persona and then crafting content that will resonate and grow your audience. People only see the young man or woman who hit the 3-point shot to beat the buzzer.

Overnight success is built one small step at a time with diligence and hard work. However you choose to find clients, cold-calling, advertising, or networking for referrals, it will be hard. Whatever social media platform you choose to master, the learning curve will be hard, and once you have it mastered the algorithm will change. Commit to the process and find a way to have fun doing the work. A couple in my network are marriage coaches and they help people divorce-proof their relationship. I want to borrow their tagline: "If it's not fun you're not doing it right!"

FINAL THOUGHTS

YOUR VOICE AMPLIFIED: EMBRACING YOUR ROLE AS A LEADER AND STORYTELLER

> "If your actions inspire others to dream more, learn more, do more, and become more, you are a leader."- Simon Sinek

No matter what title you've given yourself - founder, owner, CEO, etc. because you started your business you are a leader. You've chosen the challenging path of entrepreneurship as a way to earn your living. You are well aware your customers need to be able to learn about your services so that you exchange your expertise in the form of a product or service for their money. One of the best ways to get known is with a powerful presentation describing what you do, delivered in person or on camera. Yet, for many, public speaking is a huge stressor. Maybe you remember Jerry Seinfeld's stitch about the fear of public speaking. The essence of his routine was if you attend a wake, the person giving the eulogy would rather be the person in the casket. Yes, research has found most would rather die than speak in public. But not you. Not anymore because you've been following along, doing the work and you are ready to step out and share your message.

Will it be stressful? Yes! Of course, your journey toward speaking excellence will be sprinkled with stress. Because we are human the butterflies in our stomachs will take flight, no matter how many times we appear before an audience. Stress is an inevitable companion that tags along, regardless of the path we take. But what if we could transform the way we perceive and handle this ubiquitous guest? Let's explore how we can turn stress from a foe into an ally.

In the 1950s, Dr. Hans Seley first introduced us to the concept of stress: eustress, the good; and distress, the bad. It's a fascinating duality that pervades our lives. Eustress, often referred to as "good stress," is characterized by feelings of excitement, motivation, and fulfillment. It's the type of stress that propels us forward, fueling our ambition and driving us toward our goals.

On the other hand, distress, or "bad stress," is the type of stress we typically associate with negativity and discomfort. It manifests as anxiety, frustration, and overwhelm, hindering our ability to function effectively and undermining our well-being.

What makes stress so fascinating is its dual nature—it's neither inherently positive nor negative. Instead, its impact largely depends on how we perceive and manage it. When harnessed effectively, stress can catalyze growth and achievement, pushing us out of our comfort zones and propelling us toward success.

However, when we allow our focus to shift to the wrong aspects—dwelling on potential failures, fixating on uncontrollable factors, or succumbing to self-doubt—even good stress can quickly spiral into distress. It's a delicate balance that requires mindfulness and self-awareness to navigate effectively.

Understanding the nuances of stress empowers us to harness its positive aspects while easing its negative effects. We can cultivate resilience, use healthy coping strategies, and maintain perspective that can transform stress from a debilitating force into a powerful ally in life.

When you bring to mind the vision of yourself standing on a podium before a sea of smiling faces patiently awaiting your presentation, how do you feel? I hope that you feel more confident in your ability to conquer the crowd. Armed with your story you can successfully navigate the stormy seas of presenting on and off camera to connect with your ideal audience. You now have a message that resonates with them, and you are beginning to share it to make a difference in the lives of the people who need you and your work.

There is power in reframing any situation. Our ability to shift perspective can never be underestimated, especially when it comes to managing stress. Take the legendary Thomas Alva Edison, for instance. At the ripe age of 67, he witnessed his plant being consumed by a raging inferno. Instead of succumbing to despair, he saw it as a spectacle to behold and invited his family to witness the blaze. It's this remarkable reframing of a potentially traumatic event that we can all learn from. Rather than allowing stress to accelerate our heart rates and flood our bodies with stress hormones, we can choose to watch the flames with a sense of awe and curiosity.

In the preceding pages, we discussed a variety of techniques to stay calm when delivering our message. Mindfulness and breathing techniques are well-trodden paths for controlling stress hormones. While I won't dive deeply into those here, consider this a gentle reminder of their power. However, there's another key element in our arsenal against stress—tenacity.

There's a compelling image that's stayed with me over the years: the tenacity of a weed. As any gardener knows, weeds are the epitome of resilience. They grow, they spread, and no matter how many times we pull them out, they spring back with relentless vigor. In many ways, managing stress requires the same dogged determination.

Within the context of business, whether we're wrestling with client acquisition, refining systems, and processes, or simply keeping the lights on, we need the tenacity of those persistent weeds. It's about rising, day after day, and embracing the repetitive nature of success and stress management. It's about finding our unique keys to reframe stress and committing to that reframing process, over and over and over again.

As you continue down the path of speaking excellence, please - stay strong, stay mindful, and above all, stay tenacious.

No matter the size of your business, no matter what stage of business growth, no matter the size of your email list or social media following you have influence. Take the role of being an "influencer" seriously because the words you choose and the actions you take will have an impact on those you serve. As John Maxwell reminds us, "Leadership is influence, nothing more, nothing less. Additionally, leadership is about serving others. Of course, you started your business to have time freedom and financial freedom, it is also the freedom to serve others in a way that is symbiotic, serving the customer and serving you." As Zig Ziglar, speaker, author, and salesman extraordinaire once said, "You can get anything you want if you help enough other people get what they want." As an entrepreneur, we are here to serve. Dr. Ivan Misner built his entire fortune on the philosophy of "Givers Gain" and Bob Berg wrote a wonderful book, The Go-Giver, about a young man hungry for success who learned a simple change in focus from getting to giving brought him more success than he could imagine.

Adopt the practice of giving first. Give without expectation of anything in return directly from the person you are serving. When I first became involved in a networking group, I showed up expecting the members of the group to refer business to me. It wasn't until I learned to change my thinking and attended the meetings with the idea of listening to the needs of my fellow networkers and seeing who in my circle of influence, I could connect them to that may be a good customer or referral partner. I learned the reciprocity of giving business referrals does not come back directly to the person I gave to, but it does come back. Begin the practice of listening and looking for people to connect, make the introduction, and then step out of the way. You'll be surprised how many people will start to do this for you.

Several years ago I was enrolled in a coaching program and the woman who led it would often say being an entrepreneur is like getting a PhD in personal development. How true! The success of your practice all starts and ends with you, and you will learn lessons no formal education or classroom could teach. Be open to learning and growth. Remember the acronym for **FAIL** – **F**irst **A**ttempt **I**n **L**earning I wrote about in an early chapter. We can take a lesson from Thomas Edison in his many attempts to create the incandescent light bulb "I have not failed. I've just found 10,000 ways that won't work." Model his persistence.

There are countless stories of now-famous people who encountered setbacks along the way. Don't believe me? Put that last sentence in the search bar of

Google and see what comes up. I'll bet you will learn about Walt Disney, basketball great Michael Jordan who was cut from his high school team, and Paul Orfalea the founder of Kinkos acquired by FedEx Corp in 2004. Early in Paul's entrepreneurial journey, he began by turning the needs and problems of his customers into his business solution. His philosophy "Own It: Thinking Like an Owner in Business and Life" is what helped him overcome dyslexia and attention deficit hyperactivity disorder. Everyone will encounter challenges. It is who we become when addressing these challenges that will allow us to expand and grow. We are, after all, human beings, not human doings.

Your unique story is the compilation of the trials you've faced, learned from, and applied that learning to grow and expand your life. It is probably the reason behind your work. Toyota originated The Five Whys technique as a fundamental part of their problem-solving approach. While this technique is indeed a fascinating approach to problem-solving it is also a model for digging deeper into almost anything. Several years ago I participated in a coaching program called Biz Club and the founding coach encouraged us to follow a similar process. She recommended exercise for deep introspection. Set aside 30 to 60 minutes to write interrupted. Take out your journal or piece of paper or open a document on your computer and ask the question – ***Why?*** Repeat it until you've narrowed down your answer. Start with one of the sample questions listed here.

Why do you want to do the work you do?

Why do you want to serve the people you serve?

Why is it important?

Why will you benefit from doing the work?

Why will people benefit from working with you?

Starting with the first question - Why do you do the work you do? After each answer, dig a little deeper with the why. The series of questions could look like this: *Why does your work matter? Why does it make a difference in the world? Why is it important to make a difference in the world? Why will the world be a better place because of your work?*

What follows are my questions and answers when I did this exercise in February of 2023.

1. Why do I want to create a money-making side hustle?

To prove to myself that I can create a business enterprise that is successful. Also so I can replace my full-time income and do the work I believe I am here on planet earth to do. So I can be a role model for others.

2. Why do you need to prove it to yourself?

Because I failed in the past, and I wanted to turn all the lessons I've learned in an act on them and find a new way to think about past business experiences.

3. Why do you want to think differently about failure?

So I can be motivated to try again and find what works.

4. Why do you want to find what works?

To have an income that moves me towards financial independence. So I can serve the people I am meant to serve. So I can give back and make a positive impact with my work and make a difference in the lives of the clients I serve.

5. Why do you want to have financial independence?

So that I can save for the future and give money to causes I feel are important.

6. Why do you want to give to causes?

Tony Robbins said giving is living and I want to make a difference for people.

7. Why do you want to leave a legacy?

So that I feel accomplished to look back and say I did it! I took action and created something helpful to people. To leave the world a better place because I've lived on this planet.

This is a great exercise to help you gain clarity around your goals and the vision you have for your business and your life. It is not a one-and-done, revisit it often to remind yourself of the importance of your work and the reason you showed up here on earth in the first place.

STAYING IN TOUCH WITH YOU AUDIENCE

Any time you give a presentation your goal is to move your audience to action and capture their information to grow your contact list. If you are at an in-person event you can collect information in one of two ways.

1. Create a document to distribute to your audience that can serve two purposes, one part is for them, the other for you. I set mine up with a perforation down the middle, so they keep one half, and you get the other. If you are not at the point in your business to make that investment, have two. The part they keep has the key points of your talk and your contact info, the half you keep has a place for them to write their contact info along with a comment you can use, with permission, as a testimonial. You'll find a sample on the resource page of the book's website.

As you end your presentation, guide your audience through filling it out. You must take them step by step through completing the form. Failure to do so will not get you the result you want – names and contacts for your database. You can use language such as: You've been a fabulous audience today and I'd love to stay connected. To do that I need your information. The handout you have at your table will accomplish that. Please get your pen and let me know the following by filling in the blanks: one idea you liked, check the box if I can quote you on my website. The next part asks them for their contact information in exchange for your freebie. Then add a box that asks if they'd have a call to see how you can support them. Name the call, many people today know that a discovery call is code for a sales call. Offer value, if they give you 30 minutes of their time, you'll give them an analysis of where they are now and how they can move forward using the information you shared in your talk. And one last box to check, do you know another organization that could use this valuable information, if so, I'll follow up to learn more. Leave them at your place and I'll be around after to pick them up. I know from personal experience the times I did not follow the process of guiding audience members step by step in filling out the form were the times very few people filled out the form.

2. Create a QR code that does the same thing. Instruct your audience to use their mobile device, scan the code, and step them through completing the form you've created to capture the same information described above.

You now have a collection of warm leads, don't let them grow cold. Within 24 hours of returning to your office, enter the data into your CRM, send any giveaway you've promised to send, and follow up on places to share your message. Be sure to stay in touch with your email drip campaign developed to keep your audience engaged with your message and eventually buy your product or service.

VIRTUAL EVENTS

Most scheduling platforms have a way to register audience members in advance that will allow you to capture their contact information. Once you have their email address you can create a series of follow-up messages, often referred to as a drip campaign, to encourage them to book a call or buy your course directly through a link. Why is it called a drip campaign? Because you're sending small bits of information over time, just like a dripping faucet will fill up a sink one drop at a time. You will be staying in touch with them until they either buy or subscribe from your list.

The way we interact with our audience on social platforms is changing. It is no longer enough to like, share, and subscribe. You want to create interaction and build a relationship. Respond to comments, ask questions, and encourage dialogue. Show genuine interest in your followers' thoughts and experiences, and make them feel heard and valued.

Share your story. Stories have a unique ability to captivate and connect with audiences on an emotional level. Share personal anecdotes, client success stories, or behind-the-scenes glimpses of your business to humanize your brand and foster deeper connections with your audience.

Interactive content such as polls, quizzes, and interactive stories can be highly engaging and encourage active participation from your audience. It provides an opportunity for them to express their opinions, share insights, and interact with your brand in a fun and interactive way.

Encourage your followers to create and share content

related to your brand or products. User-generated content not only serves as social proof but also fosters a sense of community and belonging among your audience. Repost and acknowledge user-generated content to show appreciation and strengthen relationships with your followers.

Let's say you're a wellness coach and you want to engage your audience on social media. Instead of simply posting tips and advice, you decide to host a weekly "Wellness Wednesday" series where you invite your followers to share their favorite healthy recipes, workout routines, or self-care practices. You create a dedicated hashtag (#WellnessWednesdayWith[YourName]) and encourage participants to use it when sharing their wellness tips. Each week, you feature selected submissions on your profile, along with a shout out to the contributor. This not only encourages engagement and participation but also creates a sense of community and fosters connections among your followers who share a common interest in wellness.

Track user engagement with this data. You can also encourage them to visit your website to download your free offer in exchange for their email. Sometimes referred to as an ethical bribe, it is a way to build a following to contact. Unlike followers on a specific site, you own your email list.

NETWORKING EVENTS

Virtual events are more and more popular and since you won't have a physical business card to hand out have a document with your relevant details ready to copy and paste into the chat. Often this is your name, website, email, link to your free offer or registration link to your upcoming event.

Of course if you are in person you can ask for their business card. Make a note of your conversation on the back of their card and let them know you will follow up. Of course not everyone you meet will be a good connection so follow up won't be necessary. Keep control and schedule the meeting. Someone once said: *the fortune is in the follow up*. And it is so true, I've left many an event with a promise of follow up from someone that I never hear from again. I soon learned I needed to take control and scheduled calendar reminders for outreach after the event. As discussed in the earlier chapter on networking, your goal is to decide: is this person someone to whom you can refer business to and vice versa.

SEEK FEEDBACK AND MAKE ADJUSTMENTS

Along with your step-by-step plan for integrating self-promotion strategies into your business routine establish a feedback loop for continuous improvement. The audience feedback form discussed earlier is one form of feedback. LinkedIn will give analytics: the number of followers, post impressions, profile viewers and search appearance. Create a Facebook and Instagram business page to take advantage of the results from your efforts across these platforms. Develop a way to measure the revenue generated from your presentations. The number of connections you've made when networking along with the number of referrals you've given in to your network. It will be up to you to determine the key metrics you will measure in your business and along with a. Make it a practice to review the data at the end of each month, each quarter, and each year. Think of any plan you build for your business as a living document, one that you will use as a tool to help guide decisions. After all, as Yogi Berra once said, "If you don't know where you are going, you'll end up somewhere else."

EXPECT THE UNEXPECTED

Your story is ever changing, as you learn and grow you will have more to share with your audience. Think of life as a road trip and you are in the driver's seat. The trip will be filled with twists and turns, peaks and valleys, smooth freeways, and bumpy dirt roads. Embrace each part of your trip because you will never pass this way again. You may come across a roadblock and have to take an alternative route. Your vehicle might break down and the needed repairs cause delays. The road of entrepreneurship is filled with potholes, detours, and delays. When we don't reach our destination as we had planned, it can cause angst and frustration. Instead of focusing on what went wrong, focus on what has gone right. The distance traveled, instead of the point on the map you desire to end up. It is also filled with views of spectacular sunsets, lofty mountain vistas and verdant green valleys. Stop and enjoy the scenery. Celebrate each mile driven along the way, knowing there is more to come. Using speaking to promote your product or service is all about the journey rather than reaching any destination.

Some of the more well-known public speakers like Tony Robbins, Brene Brown, and Marie Forleo use speaking as a way to continually grow their influence and their business. There are others less well known that do the same thing, and you can too.

- **Sarah Johnson:** Known as "The Briefcase Coach" on LinkedIn has over 900,000 followers and hosts regular speaking events at local community centers and networking groups. Through her engaging presentations on topics such as personal branding and career development, Sarah attracts clients to her coaching services and workshops. Sarah found her passion for helping others navigate their professional paths after experiencing her own career challenges. After working in corporate environments for several years,

Sarah realized she wanted to make a more direct impact on individuals' lives. Drawing on her own experiences of career transitions and personal development, she decided to pursue coaching as a means to empower others to find fulfillment and success in their careers. Sarah's journey led her to host speaking events where she shares her insights and strategies for personal branding, career advancement, and overcoming obstacles in the job market.

- **Jason Patel:** An educational consultant and founder of Transition, a company specializing in college admissions counseling, Jason created his business based on his own struggles and triumphs during the college application process. As a first-generation college student, Jason faced numerous challenges navigating the complexities of college admissions. However, his perseverance and determination ultimately led him to secure acceptance into a prestigious university. Recognizing the need for personalized guidance and support for students facing similar challenges, Jason founded Transition, his college admissions consulting company. Through speaking engagements at high schools and community events, Jason shares his firsthand knowledge and expertise to demystify the college application process and empower students to achieve their academic goals.

- **Emily Chen:** A nutritionist and wellness coach, Emily Chen hosts free seminars and workshops at health food stores and community centers. Her passion for nutrition and wellness stems from her own journey to overcome health challenges and achieve balance in her life. After experiencing the transformative power of adopting a healthy lifestyle, Emily felt compelled to share her knowledge and insights with others. She pursued education and training in nutrition coaching and holistic wellness practices, eventually launching her own coaching practice. Through her informative presentations on topics such as mindful eating and holistic wellness, Emily establishes herself as a trusted authority in her field and generates interest in her nutrition coaching programs and meal planning services.
- **David Nguyen:** A financial advisor and founder of WealthWise Financial Planning, David Nguyen's path to financial advising was shaped by his own experiences navigating the complexities of personal finance and wealth management. Growing up in a family where financial literacy was not prioritized, David

> witnessed firsthand the impact of financial uncertainty and instability. Determined to break the cycle of financial insecurity, David pursued education and training in finance and investment management. Armed with knowledge and expertise, he founded WealthWise Financial Planning with the mission of helping individuals and families achieve financial security and prosperity. Through speaking engagements at local libraries and business networking events, David shares his insights and strategies for retirement planning, investment management, and financial goal-setting, empowering attendees to take control of their financial futures.

Remember everyone starts somewhere, the important point is to start. The only impossible journey is the one you never begin. Long ago I clipped this poem and refer to it when I need a reminder about what is important in life and to be certain I'm having fun along the way. Attributed to Nadine Stair written at age 85 has always been one of my favorites. Although Wikipedia suggests the author was actually a man and Nadine Stair did not really exist, I still like the message: a good reminder to live in the moment and embrace what is before us instead of worrying about what might happen tomorrow and criticizing what did happen yesterday.

If I Had My Life to Live Over

I'd dare to make more mistakes next time. I'd relax. I would limber up.

I would be sillier than I have been this trip. I would take fewer things seriously.

I would take more chances. I would take more trips.

I would climb more mountains and swim more rivers. I would eat more ice cream and less beans.

I would perhaps have more actual troubles, but I'd have fewer imaginary ones.

You see, I'm one of those people who live sensibly and sanely hour after hour, day after day.

Oh, I've had my moments and if I had it to do over again, I'd have more of them. In fact, I'd try to have nothing else. Just moments. One after another, instead of living so many years ahead of each day.

I've been one of those people who never go anywhere without a thermometer, a hot water bottle, a raincoat, and a parachute.

If I had my life to live over, I would start barefoot earlier in the spring and stay that way later in the fall.

If I had it to do again, I would travel lighter next time. I would go to more dances. I would ride more merry-go-rounds. I would pick more daisies.

MOVING FORWARD

Your goal is excellence, not perfection. As speaker Les Brown reminds us; "Shoot for the moon even if you miss, you'll land among the stars." My final piece of advice, dear reader, is to find opportunities to speak on a regular basis. Leverage the value in showing up in a way that is genuine to connect with the people you want to serve. There are any number of platforms that offer invaluable opportunities to connect with potential clients, showcase your expertise, and establish yourself as a trusted authority in your field.

As you embark on your journey to grow your business, I encourage you to actively seek out speaking opportunities and networking events in your local community and beyond. Whether it's attending industry conferences, joining professional organizations, or participating in Toastmasters meetings, each interaction presents a chance to expand your network and amplify your message.

Remember, every conversation, presentation, and connection is an opportunity to make a lasting impression and attract new clients. So, step out of your comfort zone, embrace the power of storytelling, and seize every opportunity to share your message with the world.

By actively engaging in speaking and networking

events, you'll not only elevate your visibility and credibility but also create meaningful connections that can propel your coaching business to new heights. So, go forth with confidence, enthusiasm, and a commitment to making a lasting impact through your words and connections.

CONCLUSION

As I write this final segment I have you, my dear reader, in my mind's eye, now ready to embrace sharing your story before an audience to build your following and grow your business. Congratulations on doing the work it takes to move forward and step into being a confident speaker. Growth emerges from facing difficulties and overcoming obstacles. The challenge of learning to be a powerful speaker will push you beyond your comfort zones. It will lead you down the path of personal development and transformation. Even when change feels uncomfortable, it can lead to positive outcomes if we embrace it with patience and resilience. Take the opportunity set before you to be the best speaker you can be, welcome that challenge and view it as an opportunity for growth!

At any given moment a lot of chemistry is happening in your body. In your brain, neurotransmitters like **dopamine**, **serotonin**, and **norepinephrine** waltz across synapses, shaping your mood, memory, and motivation. They're the secret choreographers behind your emotions and cognitive functions. It is this intricate dance of neurons, neurotransmitters, and feedback loops that ensures our survival and well-being. In order to maintain homeostasis, your brain would prefer you to stay right where you are, safe, snug, and comfortable without putting any effort toward change or self-improvement. When you put new demands on your system, such as speaking in front of an audience, your brain will send signals to you questioning the need for such action. Ideally, we want to find the balance between self-discovery and self-acceptance in our everyday life. And maybe it isn't so much balance between the two as it is finding harmony. It is like playing a stringed instrument, pulling the string too tight will cause it to break, not enough tension and there is no music. Public speaking may provide the same heart pounding experience that thrill seekers, who do things like sky-dive, heli-ski or bungee jump seeking out experiences that push their limits and ignite their passion for adventure! Step out of your comfort zone and into your challenge zone, your audience is waiting to hear from you.

Imagine a grand emporium known as "The Speaker's Boutique." Its doors swing open wide, inviting in speakers of all kinds, from beginners to seasoned professionals. Any topic is welcome too, from business and money to spirituality and wellbeing. As you step inside you notice a sign above the counter shimmering with golden letters: "Creating Your Signature Story, One Thread at a Time."

Inside, the air is filled with anticipation. Shelves lined the walls, each laden with bolts of fabric, colors as diverse as any place on earth. The Storyteller's Boutique offers more than cloth, it is a place of magic, the color and fiber of imagination.

You initially travel down the aisle of beginnings where the fabrics whisper of first steps, tentative and raw. Cottons of innocence, silks of curiosity, and linens of wonder lay side by side. See yourself reaching out to touch them. Maybe it's a bolt of sky-blue satin. Grasping the fabric between your fingers and feeling its softness you imagine a new beginning, the promise of untold stories.

Beyond the aisles, velvet curtains lead to private fitting rooms with a sign above each room: "Opening Lines," "Sharing Your Why" "Confident Conclusions." This is the section where you don the persona of your ideal client. Stepping into their pain adjusting the mirrors, seeking the right angle when sharing your story. As you twirl about in front of the glass, you'll examine the fit. Asking "Is the setting snug or too spacious?" The mirror reflects back questions, urging you to explore further. You soon realize it is a magical mirror that will listen and whisper back advice to alter your words. "Try a dash of humor," it will advise. "Or perhaps a touch of melancholy." It will encourage you to test a variety of tones and inflections to create the perfect outfit.

Your next stop will be the Embroidery Corner of Details. Here, spools of thread hang like rainbows. Allowing you to thread needles and embroidered details onto their narratives. Maybe a scar from a forgotten battle or the scent of cinnamon to bring forth a found memory. The fabric of your presentation will absorb these intricacies, becoming richer, more textured.

The final stop will be the runway of sharing where you will emerge from the fitting room with your presentation tailored and hemmed. Much like a top fashion model you will step onto the glittering runway and strut confidently to the erupting applause and gasps of recognition from your audience. "I've felt that" they will whisper. "I've been there."

And so, dear reader, remember: Creating your signature story to share is like trying on clothes. Each word, each scene, is a fabric waiting to be stitched. So step into the fitting room, adjust the mirrors, and find your unique style. The world awaits your creation—a masterpiece sewn from threads of the heart.

Be sure to visit my website for free resources and downloads. https://www.lesliefiorenzo.com/book/resources

AFTERWORD

The journey to finding your voice and sharing your authentic message takes courage and commitment. It is my hope these pages have inspired you to move past fear and embrace the power of your story, let me leave you with this - don't wait for the "right" time. There is no better moment than right now.

Too often, we fall into the trap of delaying our growth, believing that someday the circumstances will be perfect for stepping into the spotlight. But that day may never arrive unless you create it for yourself today. Your business cannot thrive, and your impact cannot reverberate if you remain the best-kept secret in town.

Remember, any worthwhile change requires patience and persistence. Avoid becoming discouraged if progress seems incremental at first. Approach this journey with a mindset of taking one small, purposeful step forward each day. Those steps will compound over time, establishing unshakable self-assurance and an ability to captivate any audience.

I encourage you to take tangible action immediately to improve your speaking skills - whether delivering presentations in-person, speaking confidently on camera, or working the room at networking events. Seek out groups of like-minded individuals who can offer accountability and support. Or invest in hiring a coach who can provide professional guidance tailored to your unique needs. The investment you make in yourself now will pay exponential dividends in the future.

Most importantly, embrace the art of storytelling as you put yourself out there. Appeals rooted in facts and figures alone can only go so far. But by sharing your authentic experiences and insights through a well-crafted narrative, you tap into the core of human connection. People don't just remember information - they remember how that information made them feel. Make them feel inspired, understood, and empowered through your story.

You've been given a powerful gift - a unique voice, perspective, and message that only you can share with the world. Have the courage and conviction to wield that gift boldly. Your journey to impacting lives, serving your clients fully, and building a wildly successful business begins right here.

Step forward, find your voice, and watch your world change.

REFERENCES

CHAPTER 1

1. https://www.smartinsights.com/digital-marketing-platforms/video-marketing/video-marketing-statistics-to-know/In and https://www.oyova.com/blog/the-rise-of-video-marketing/
2. https://www.oyova.com/blog/the-rise-of-video-marketing/s
3. https://blog.hubspot.com/marketing/video-marketing-report#goals
4. https://www.google.com/url?q=https://www.healthline.com/health/rewiring-your-brain&sa=D&source=docs&ust=1708810421324216&usg=AOvVaw1cF6pI6BxPmLQ4dcHslM9g
5. https://www.google.com/url?q=https://www.today.com/health/your-brain-cant-swipe-hear-same-time-scans-show-t60356&sa=D&source=docs&ust=1708810421348311&usg=AOvVaw29AHLscI2ugvAXo2-Ne_20

CHAPTER 3

1. https://www.huffpost.com/entry/probability-being-born_b_877853
2. https://www.cnn.com/2015/12/04/health/unique-body-parts/index.html

CHAPTER 4

1. https://www.nps.gov/places/000/national-historic-oregon-trail-center-trail-ruts.htm#:~:text=The%20trek%20across%20Virtue%20Flats,on%20the%20interpretive%20center's%20grounds

CONNECTING AND ENGAGING WITH YOUR AUDIENCE

1. https://www.entrepreneur.com/starting-a-business/the-true-failure-rate-of-small-businesses/361350

ABOUT THE AUTHOR

Early in her career Leslie belonged to a businesswomen's group, and they held a speaking contest. First prize was $100. She entered, prepared and was disappointed when she didn't win first prize. She didn't even place in the top 5! Her mentor who was in the audience, gave her the following feedback: "You had a death grip the podium, did you think it was going to run away? You stumbled over your words and the two stories you told didn't connect to the topic." She was devastated. It was all she could do to not cry on the way home in a car full of other women. This experience fueled her determination to conquer her fears, create stories that make an impact and craft a presentation that would wow the audience. Fast forward 10 years and her then employer sent her to present the company's safety program at an industry conference. This time the prize was based on the impact of the program not the presentation, yet when people approached Leslie afterward and gave her complements on her delivery and the stories she shared; she knew she'd moved well beyond that timid young woman losing a speech contest years before. In the years since she earned her competent Toastmaster certificate; graduated from the Michigan Speaker's Association Professional Track Program and has spoken to thousands of business owners about how to grow their business using referral marketing. Her desire it to help you find your voice so you can share your unique story to grow your business.

Leslie's unique perspective and approach comes from 30 years spent in corporate environments as a human resources professional. A lifelong learner, she has achieved a number of certifications including a facilitator with Conversational Management, Thera-Rising, IPV Consulting and DISC based learning tools. Her commitment to helping others grow and develop led her to teach human resources, business, and marketing courses as an adjunct faculty member at Davenport University and as an independent consultant with Business Network International.

Leslie received her bachelor's degree from Spring Arbor College and her master's in human resource development from Western Michigan University. She and her husband live in Wyoming, Michigan. When she is not serving her clients she enjoys daily walks in her neighborhood, yoga and from mid-April to mid-October each year, she and her husband enjoy spending time in their travel trailer that does not travel. They have a seasonal site at a campground on the Thornapple River.

Be sure to visit my website for free resources and downloads. https://www.lesliefiorenzo.com/book/resources

www.ingramcontent.com/pod-product-compliance
Lightning Source LLC
Chambersburg PA
CBHW071630200326
41519CB00012BA/2230
9781068683831